SUN, WIND, AND LIGHT

ARCHITECTURAL DESIGN STRATEGIES

SUN, WIND, AND LIGHT

ARCHITECTURAL DESIGN STRATEGIES

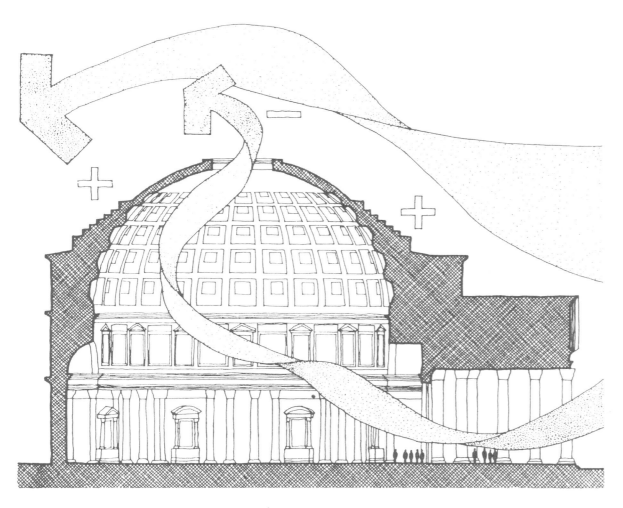

G. Z. BROWN
Department of Architecture
University of Oregon

ILLUSTRATIONS
V. CARTWRIGHT
Department of Architecture
Kansas State University

JOHN WILEY & SONS

New York Chichester Brisbane Toronto Singapore

Library of Congress Cataloging in Publication Data:

Brown, G. Z.
   Sun, wind, and light

   Bibliography: p.
   Includes index.
   1. Architecture and energy conservation.

I. Title.
NA2542.3.B76   1985   720'.47   84-29117
ISBN 0-471-89506-7
ISBN 0-471-82063-6 (pbk.)

Printed in the United States of America

10 9

To ASB: for what it's worth

PREFACE

My purpose in writing this book is to help architectural designers who are not energy experts understand the energy consequences of their most basic design decisions and to give them information so that they can use energy issues to generate form rather than simply as limits that must be accommodated. It is not that energy is important in and of itself, but that the processes of making energy that depend on fossil fuels are damaging to the natural environment to which we are inextricably bound. So, in the long run at least, environmental cost equals social cost; conversely, environmental benefit equals social benefit. It seems then that energy issues should be of professional concern to architects, whose goal is to improve the quality of life.

If energy is the concern, why cover only daylighting and passive solar heating and cooling? Certainly energy use in architecture can and should be addressed more broadly than it is in this book. My reason for narrowing the focus is to concentrate on the relationship between architectural *form* and energy use. Therefore, some important energy issues that don't have major architectural form consequences have been excluded. It also means that some architectural concerns have been addressed from an extremely narrow perspective. Daylighting, for example, which

some say is the essence of architecture, is treated simply as a strategy for reducing electric lighting levels. It is because daylighting is of such broad concern in architecture that this narrow perspective is valuable: it lets the designer know both the good and bad energy consequences of certain approaches to daylighting and shows how those consequences change with building type and climate.

I have concentrated on *passive* means of heating, cooling, and lighting because they are more closely tied to building form than active systems are. However, the line between passive and active systems has not been rigorously drawn, and many of the illustrations are hybrid in nature. I have concentrated on heating, cooling, and lighting because they are the most important energy uses in buildings, and because they demonstrate a strong influence on form. My preoccupation with the connections between architectural form and energy is not because I think that all energy issues should profoundly affect architectural form but because architectural form can profoundly affect energy use. Those effects should be known and taken into consideration in the design process.

Throughout this book I have tried to credit original sources for data and ideas even if they appear here greatly revised. However, much of this information is of my own devising, so no references are cited.

I would like to acknowledge the people who helped make this book possible. First, I want to thank the students who have been in my architectural design studios. It was through their eyes that I first saw the need for a book structured like this one. It has been through their struggles that I have learned to identify what is meaningful and useful at the beginning of the design process. Four former students, Jeff Stark, Marla Fritzlen, Don Harton,

and Ronda Thompson, did research that was crucial to this project. Don Harton also prepared and tested pieces of the analysis section on generic heating and cooling patterns.

A major influence on this book came from the curriculum development project initiated by the University of Pennsylvania and the U.S. Department of Energy. I would particularly like to thank Harrison Fraker, Don Prowler, and Bob Shibley. Several documents that resulted from that program have been used in this book. But more importantly, that project and the continued efforts of those individuals have gone a long way towards establishing the ongoing dialogue about energy and architecture that exists within schools of architecture today.

Since coming to the University of Oregon, I have established regular working relationships with two people, Bobby-Jo Novitski and John Reynolds, who have greatly influenced my perception of architecture. I see their influence over and over again in this book. I would like to especially thank Bobby-Jo, who has carefully reviewed the entire manuscript and has made innumerable valuable suggestions on both style and content. Without her help I would never write anything readable.

Many of the ideas in this book were first considered while Susan Ubbelohde, John Reynolds, and I were developing *INSIDEOUT, Design Procedures for Passive Environmental Technologies* for publication, and I would like to acknowledge the importance of our discussions in the development of this book.

I would also like to thank Ginger Cartwright, who illustrated the book. She has gone far beyond the role of illustrator in her suggestions on book layout and organization and thoughts about effective communication. Her familiarity with the design process and energy issues made her judgments about what should be included extremely valuable. I also want to thank her for her willingness to do far more illustrations than were originally envisioned. I would like to thank Heidi Humphrey for her thoughts on book design.

Several people within the School of Architecture and Allied Arts deserve thanks: Mary Williams, who typed the manuscript and was the first line of defense in spelling and grammar; and Jerry Finrow, Department Head, and Bill Gilland, Dean, who are generous with their release time but who, more importantly, help establish the school as an enjoyable and productive work place.

I owe a great deal to Mike Pyatok, who has helped me clarify my values about architecture and who has a systematic and rigorous way of thinking about architecture that I admire and try to emulate.

I would also like to thank Ron Kellett, who stepped in at a moment of doubt to help me restructure and reorganize and to give me encouragement.

For their thoughtful review of the manuscript and many useful suggestions, I would like to thank Susan Ubbelohde of Florida A & M, Jack Kremers of Kent State University, Harvey Bryan of the Massachusetts Institute of Technology, Bruce Haglund of the University of Idaho, and Jerry Finrow of the University of Oregon.

And last, I want to thank April Shelley Brown for her support and endless trips to the library and the copy center as the deadline drew near.

GZB

CONTENTS

PART TWO   DESIGN STRATEGIES   64

A   BUILDING GROUPS   67

CONTENTS

Rooms: Compact Organizations

Rooms: Zoned Organizations

Courtyards: Layers

Courtyards: Size and Shape

Rooms and Courtyards: Shape and Orientation

Rooms and Courtyards: Zoned Organizations

C   BUILDING PARTS   119

Walls, Roofs, and Floors: Size

Walls, Roofs, and Floors: Color

Walls and Floors: Size and Materials

Walls: Materials and Location

INTRODUCTION

A basic premise of this book is that most decisions that affect a building's energy use occur during the schematic design stage of the project. Furthermore, the effort required to implement those decisions at the beginning of the design process is small compared to the effort that would be necessary later on in the design process. Therefore, if energy issues are going to receive an appropriate level of consideration at the beginning of the design process, they must be presented in a way which is useful to the designer and fits with other things the designer is considering at that time. At first, the designer works primarily in a synthesis mode, bringing ideas together, not in an analysis mode. Therefore, information and problem analysis must be presented in a way that is generative of architectural form, that helps the designer understand how the forms generated by energy concerns fit with forms generated by other architectural issues. The schematic design stage is one in which things proceed very rapidly, involving experimentation with many ideas and combinations of ideas. The considerations are broad and conceptual rather than detailed and fine. Therefore, information should be accessible and quick to use.

It is anticipated that the users of this book will have some background in energy issues and techniques, so it does not pretend to be a complete, self-sufficient reference or textbook. These considerations have had a profound effect on the character of this book. The information presented is at a rule-of-thumb level. Its intention is to give only general ideas about architectural elements and their size and relationship to other elements. Precision of the information is sacrificed somewhat so that speed of use may be increased. The approximation methods are founded on certain assumptions about the elements under consideration. If those assumptions do not apply to the considerations of the moment, then the approximations probably won't either. So along with the speed of use comes a certain need for caution, though no more so than with many of the other concerns in the schematic stage. It is important to realize that, in order to **develop** a design based on the ideas in this book, the designer must also go to other sources.

Most of the ideas in this book are presented in a one- or two-page format. Each spread contains a statement of the idea, a brief explanation of the phenomenon and its architectural implications, and an illustration of how the idea has been used. The brevity is aimed at increasing speed of use, and the illustrations are a means of helping the designer translate ideas into architectural form.

This book is organized in three parts: analysis techniques, design strategies, and strategies for supplementing passive systems.

The first part, on analysis techniques, plays a crucial but supporting role to the second part. The analysis techniques help the designer define the context of the problem, by understanding the sun, wind, and light resources of a particular site and climate. They also help the designer understand the design problems: Are they heating, cooling, or daylighting? How do they change over the day and from season to season, and how are they affected by changes in the building's form and envelope construction? With this information the designer can form an idea of what kinds of strategies are likely to be important.

The heart of the book is the second part, on design strategies. It is the section that designers will find the most useful while formulating a basic design concept for a project. The design strategies are organized first in terms of scale: building groups, buildings, and building

parts. This helps a designer understand a particular principle like sun movement at a scale of consideration that is similar to the project. Within the scale organization, the strategies are organized by the architectural elements, such as streets, blocks, rooms, windows, and walls, and by the relationships between those elements, such as layers and zones. This approach was used because architectural elements are the common denominator of the issues under consideration at the scheming stage. They are what the designer manipulates to develop a design concept. For example, when considering the role of windows, the designer can find heating, cooling, and daylighting strategies together organized under the categories of window orientation, size, location, and shape. These strategies can be considered together and with other window considerations such as view or display.

The third part of the book, on supplements to passive systems, is the shortest, but it addresses an important consideration of how passive design strategies should be integrated with more conventional electrical and mechanical systems in buildings. This integration is complex, especially in large buildings, and could easily fill a book by itself. My intention in Part Three is to identify recurring considerations, like how to extend the heat storage capacity of passive systems, and to explain their potential architectural impact, not to give rules of thumb for sizing systems.

Readers should understand that this book deals primarily with temperate climates like those within the United States. Many of the design strategies will be useful in other climates, but there is a distinct bias towards those that address the changing nature of temperate climates rather than the more consistent needs of extremely hot or cold regions.

Also implicit in these strategies is a sun position to the south of the building that stays low in the winter sky. These assumptions are inappropriate for regions in the southern hemisphere or near the equator.

The book is organized in several ways to help the user find a particular piece of information. First, the table of contents lists all of the techniques and strategy statements under their major headings and subheadings so that in a few minutes one can get a feeling for what is covered in the entire book. The same statements occur in **bold** type at the beginning of the discussion of that technique or strategy. Each statement is followed by a subject, either heating, cooling, or daylighting, that it concerns. Within the strategy statements, the discussion of the illustration and the sizing rule of thumb are *highlighted* so that they can be easily found. Within the text, sources that contain a more detailed explanation of the idea or the example are identified by author and page number in parentheses. These sources frequently aren't the original source but are a convenient place to find more information. A complete citation for all sources mentioned in the text can be found in the bibliography.

Each section has an introductory overview and gives an example of how the techniques and strategies are related to each other and to techniques and strategies in other sections.

The book is also indexed by subject, architect, building, and selected tables and graphs so that after you've read about an idea it will be easy to retrieve. A glossary provides definitions for technical terms used in the text.

PART ONE
ANALYSIS TECHNIQUES

The purpose of Part One is to present techniques that enable the designer to understand, **before** the building is designed, how the building is likely to use energy, so that appropriate architectural design strategies for daylighting and passive solar heating and cooling can be a basic and integral part of the initial design idea. In order to formulate these analysis techniques, a distinction was made between analysis techniques, design strategies, and evaluation techniques. Analysis techniques are used *to understand the problem* and its context. They characterize the important variables and establish their relative importance. Design strategies are form-generating; they concentrate on revealing the relationship between architectural form and space and energy use. Evaluation techniques differ from analysis techniques in that they follow the design proposition. They are used to evaluate the performance of a design. While their content might be quite similar to analysis techniques, their use is fundamentally different, and their potential impact on the initial design idea is much smaller because they cannot inform that initial idea. Granted, design is a reiterative process of analysis, design, evaluation, redesign, and reevaluation. There is an opportunity for evaluation to affect design; however, the role of evaluation is always to force change in the initial idea rather than to be an integral part of its formulation. Because a building must be envisioned before its energy use can be understood, evaluation techniques have tended to play a more important role than either design strategies or analysis tools in the design process as it relates to energy use. Therefore, energy considerations have played a less formative role in the initial conception of a design than they potentially could.

The analysis techniques are subdivided into four groups: Climate as a Context (Techniques 1-10), Program and Use (Techniques 11-13), Form and Envelope (Techniques 14-16), and Combining Climate, Program, and Form (Techniques 17-19). The climate analysis techniques are directed at establishing the context. They allow the designer to determine what resources of sun, wind, and light are available on the site and how they interact over the course of the day and year. The severity of the climate can be assessed to help to determine the building's role in providing for human comfort.

The program and use analysis techniques concentrate on revealing how the type of building and the intensity and rate of use affect the rate of internal heat production and therefore the heating and cooling requirements.

The form and envelope technique show how a building's shape, size, orientation, and skin construction affect its ability to both lose and gain heat and thus affect its heating and cooling requirements.

The last section is perhaps the most important because those techniques show how the interaction of climate, program, and form affect heating and cooling requirements. Considered separately, the design implications of climate, program, and form are intuitively understandable. But when combined and considered over diurnal and seasonal cycles, they are complex and frequently counterintuitive.

While the analysis techniques can be used in any order, depending on one's design goal, a possible sequence is the following: first, a comfort analysis (Technique 10) from the climate section; then an analyis of the sun and wind (Techniques 3 and 5) as they relate to the comfort analysis; then an extension of those techniques to the site using sun position and wind flow principles (Techniques 1, 6 and 7). The designer should then proceed to the section on Combining Climate, Program, and Form. If the project is residential or residential-like in terms of size and internal loads, the next step is to use the Bioclimatic Design Strategies Analysis (Technique 17) or to see what is required to develop heating and cooling patterns (Technique 19). To generate heating and cooling patterns, analysis techniques from the Program and Use and the Form and Envelope sections are required. If daylighting is important, the section on analysis techniques from Light (Techniques 8 and 9) should be considered after the patterns have been completed.

The analysis techniques presented in this section, like the following sections on design strategies, are designed to be easy and quick to use. Therefore, their precision is quite limited in some cases, and they shouldn't be used beyond the initial stages of the design process.

A

Climate as a Context

These analysis techniques are directed at understanding a context that greatly influences how much energy buildings use, and when they use it, for heating, cooling, and lighting. The techniques are divided into five sections: sun, wind, sun and wind together, light, and comfort. All of the techniques allow the designer to evaluate the resources of the site without the inconvenience of actual on-site measurements. The methods in the sun section allow the designer to evaluate sun availability using two techniques. The first, the sun dial (Technique 1), is three-dimensional; the second, the sun path diagram (Technique 2), is graphic. The section also helps the designer estimate the amount of solar radiation available to offset low temperatures, for use later in the comfort section.

The wind techniques are geared towards translating tabular data from the weather bureau into a graphic format so that wind direction, speed, and frequency can be more easily visualized by the designer. The first two wind analysis techniques are similar, but the "wind rose" (Technique 4) emphasizes direction and frequency, while the "wind square" (Technique 5) emphasizes time of day and change over the year. The wind section ends with an explanation of principles for adjusting the weather bureau data to a particular site (Technique 6).

The sun and wind analysis section includes techniques for analyzing the combined effects of these elements on a site and helps the designer evaluate alternate locations for the building and exterior spaces.

The lighting section contains two techniques. One analyzes weather data to determine whether the conditions are clear, partly cloudy, or overcast; how they change over the year; and which condition predominates, so that minimum design conditions can be established (Technique 8). Technique 9 helps the designer determine what percentage of the year a given level of daylight will be available. The lighting section, like the sun and wind section, is primarily concerned with determining the availability of resources. It is not concerned with how those resources will be used.

The comfort section evaluates the interaction of temperature, relative humidity, radiation, and wind speed in terms of human comfort, using the bioclimatic chart (Technique 10) to suggest to the designer how the resources of the sun, wind, and light may be used. It is the single most important technique in the climate section; this chart probably should be filled in first, then supported by a wind analysis and a radiation availability analysis. These analyses can be applied to a particular site using the wind principles and sun availability techniques and summarized using the sun and wind technique. The lighting techniques are more frequently used after the desirability of daylighting has been demonstrated using Techniques 17–19 in the section Combining Climate, Program and Form, though if the bioclimatic charts indicate a substantial overheating period it is likely that daylighting will be important.

SUN

1. Simulate the changing position of sun and shade over the course of the day and throughout the year using a model and sundial.

A sundial may be used to evaluate the effects of existing site conditions, the extent of sun penetration into buildings, and the effectiveness of shading devices.

   Select the sundial with a latitude closest to that of your site. Mount a copy of the sundial on your model with north on the sundial corresponding to north on the model. Make sure that the sundial is on a horizontal (not sloping) surface. Mount a peg of the size indicated at the cross marker just below the June 21 line on the sundial. By tilting the model in the sun you can make the end of the peg's shadow fall on any intersection of the sundial. Each intersection represents the time of day and the day of the year corresponding to the two lines that meet at that intersection. When the shadow extends to a given intersection, the shadows and sun penetration in your model simulate the actual condition for that time of day and date (Lynch, p 71).

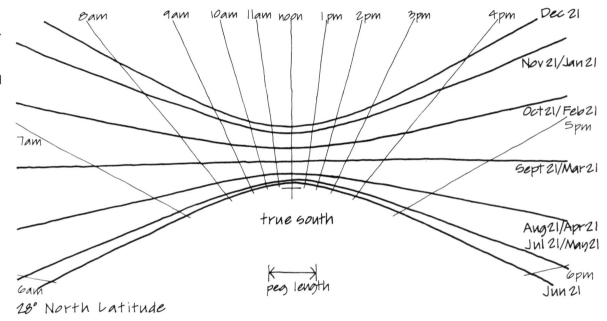

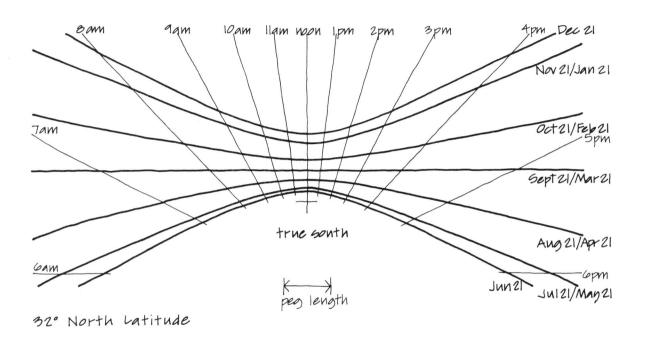

8am   9am   10am 11am noon 1pm 2pm   3pm   4pm Dec 21

Nov 21/Jan 21

7am   Oct 21/Feb 21
                                                                5pm

                                                              Sept 21/Mar 21

true south   Aug 21/Apr 21

6am   6pm
                                                        Jun 21 Jul 21/May 21

        ⊢————————⊣
          peg length

32° North Latitude

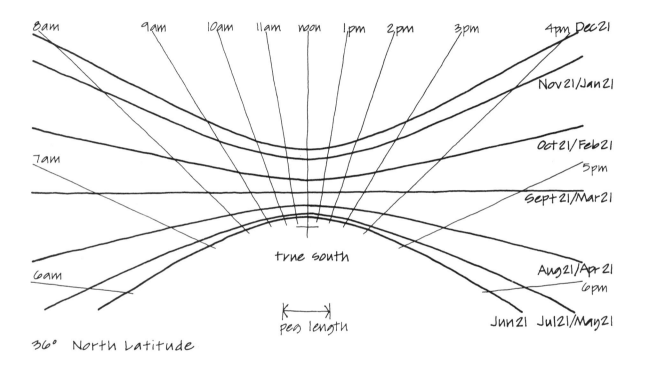

8am 9am 10am 11am noon 1pm 2pm 3pm 4pm Dec 21

Nov 21/Jan 21

Oct 21/Feb 21

7am

5pm

Sept 21/Mar 21

true south

Aug 21/Apr 21

6pm

6am

Jun 21 Jul 21/May 21

peg length

36° North Latitude

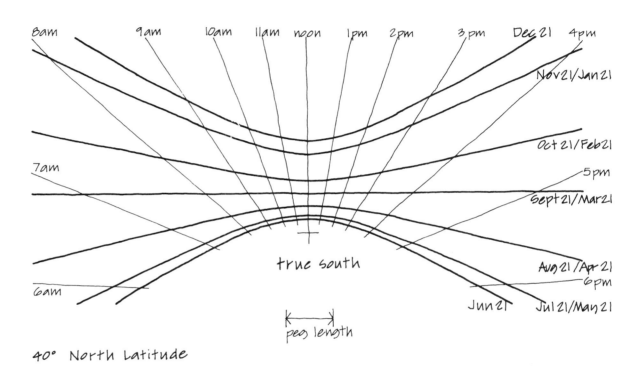

8am 9am 10am 11am noon 1pm 2pm 3pm Dec 21 4pm

Nov 21/Jan 21

Oct 21/Feb 21

7am   5pm

Sept 21/Mar 21

true south

Aug 21/Apr 21
                                                       6pm
6am   Jun 21 Jul 21/May 21

peg length

40° North Latitude

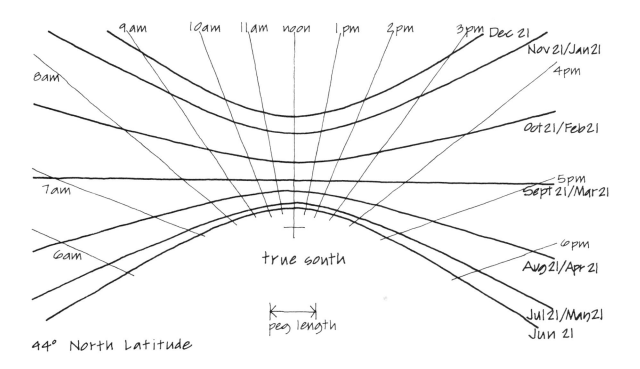

9 am   10am   11am   noon   1pm   2pm   3pm   Dec 21

Nov 21/Jan 21

8am   4pm

Oct 21/Feb 21

7am   5pm
                                                         Sept 21/Mar 21

6am   6pm

                  true south   Aug 21/Apr 21

                  |←——→| Jul 21/May 21
                  peg length   Jun 21

44° North Latitude

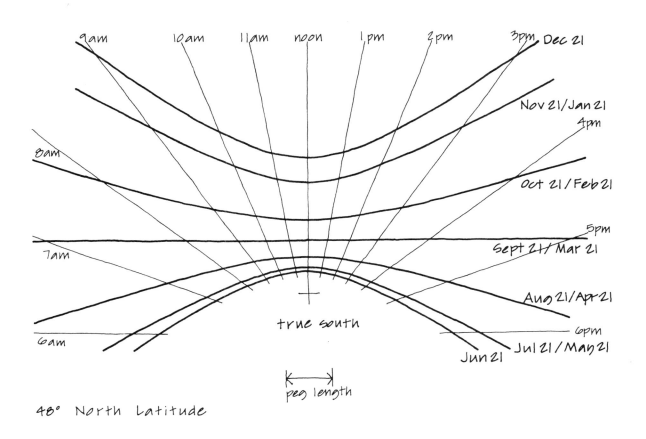

9am 10am 11am noon 1pm 2pm 3pm Dec 21

Nov 21/Jan 21

4pm

8am

Oct 21 / Feb 21

5pm

7am

Sept 21/ Mar 21

Aug 21/Apr 21

6pm

6am

Jun 21 Jul 21 / May 21

true south

peg length

48° North Latitude

SUN

2. *The times of the day and year in which the sun will be available within a particular site can be determined by drawing the existing objects on the site on a sun path diagram.*

Sun path diagrams show the path of the sun in the sky dome as projected on to a horizontal surface (Libbey-Owens-Ford, "Sun Angle Calculator"; Olgyay, p. 35; Parkard, p. 80). The heavy lines running from east to west represent the path of the sun on the 21st day of each month of the year. The heavy lines running perpendicular to the sun path lines indicate hours of the day. The light lines radiating from the center of the diagram indicate the sun's azimuth. The concentric light lines indicate the sun's altitude.

The sun path diagram for a given latitude can be used to determine the sun's position in terms of altitude and azimuth for any hour of the year. For example, to determine the sun's position at 40°N latitude, at 8 AM on Aug. 21, find the intersection of the heavy 8 AM line and the heavy sun path line for Aug. 21. Then follow the radial line that runs through the intersection to the outside circle and read the azimuth of 80° east of south. Finally, follow the concentric ring that runs through the intersection to the north/south line and read the sun altitude of 30°. Dates, times, altitudes, and azimuths may all be interpolated between values given.

Sun path diagrams for latitudes 28°–48° are provided in increments of 4°. Sun path diagrams for latitudes nearer the equator may be found in Koenigsberger et al., pp. 111, 292.

The same diagram of altitudes and azimuths may also be used to describe the position and size of objects from a particular viewpoint on a site. Trees, buildings, and hills can be described in terms of their altitude and azi-

muth from that viewpoint. By plotting them on the sun path diagram, one can tell when they will obstruct the sun and therefore shade the reference point on the site.

During overheated periods shading by such obstructions may be advantageous (Strategy 28), but during underheated periods it may be disadvantageous (Strategy 23).

The altitude and azimuth of site objects can be measured on the site using a compass and an altitude finder such as a transit or adjustable triangle, or they can be determined geometrically from a site map that shows the location and height of objects.

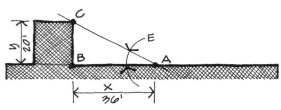

Site Section

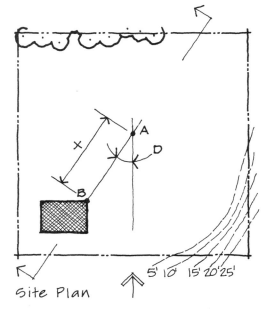

Site Plan

The example establishes a point A on the site plan, to evaluate for solar access. To determine the potential obstruction of the existing building, draw a line from point A to the corner of the building, point B. Measure the azimuth angle between that line and a due south line. Measure the distance x from point A to point B and the height y of the building. The altitude of point C, which is directly above point B on the edge of the building, can then be determined by the formula

$$\tan E = \frac{y}{x}$$

If the building height, y, is 20' and the distance from point A to B, x, is 36', the altitude of point C is 29°. The altitude of point B is 0° because it lies in the horizontal plane of the reference point A. The azimuth for both points B and C is 34° west of south.

You can now plot points B and C on the sun path diagram. The line connecting them

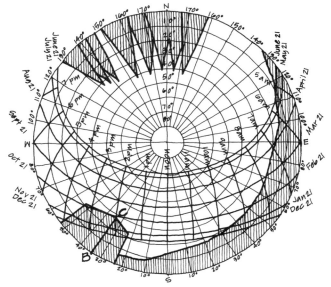

Plot of Site Obstructions

represents the building edge on the diagram. Plot enough significant points for each object on the site so that those objects can be represented on the sun path diagram. The places where the objects on the diagram cover the sun path show the times when point A will be in shade.

In the example, the building will shade point A from **about** 1:30 PM to 4 PM between Nov. 21 and Jan. 21 and 2 PM to 3 or 3:30 PM between Oct. 21 and Nov. 21 and between Jan 21 and Feb. 21. The ridge line will shade point A for some time in the morning throughout the year.

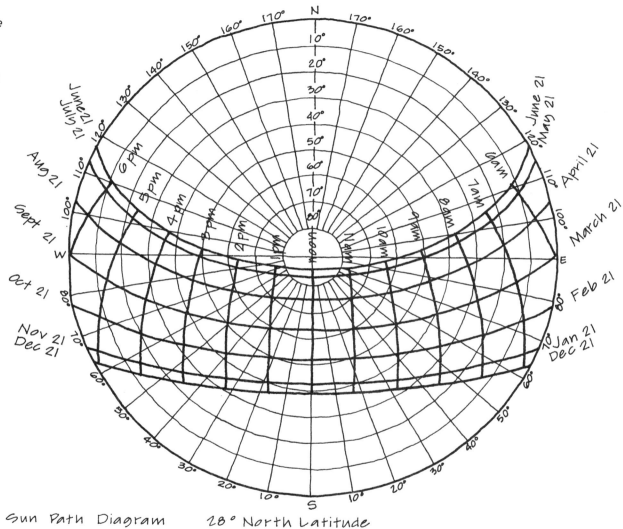

Sun Path Diagram   28° North Latitude

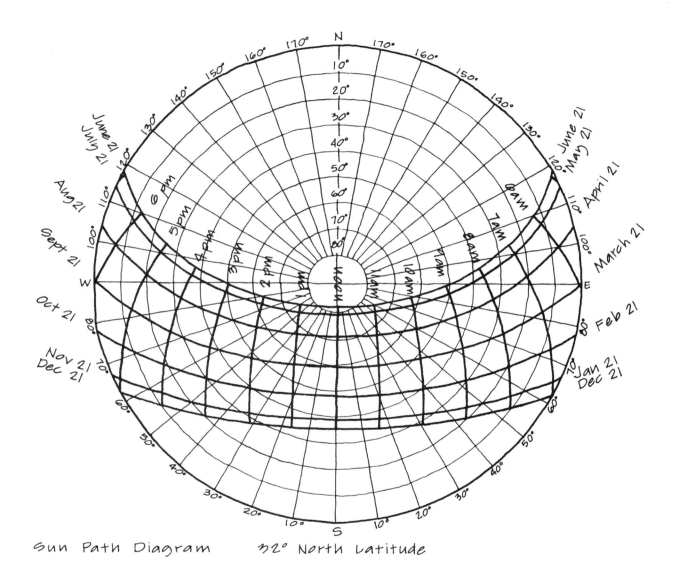

Sun Path Diagram   32° North Latitude

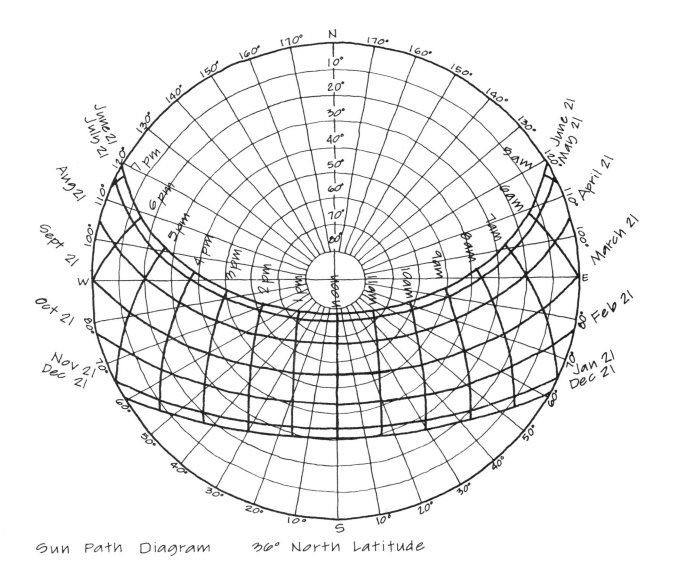

Sun Path Diagram   36° North Latitude

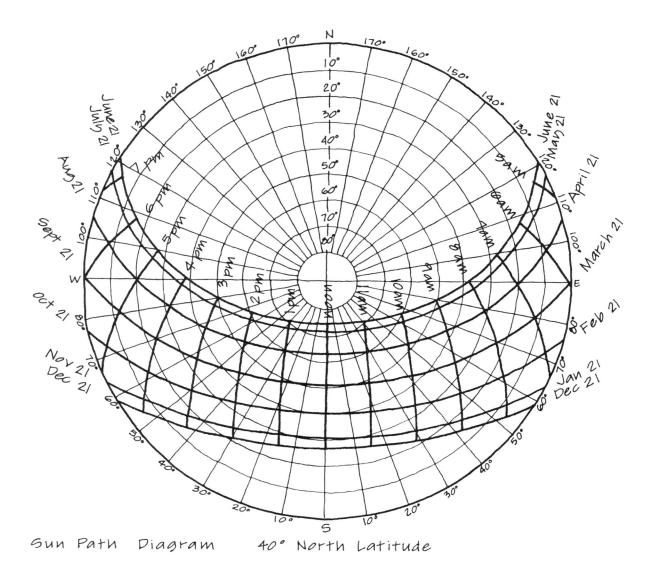

Sun Path Diagram 40° North Latitude

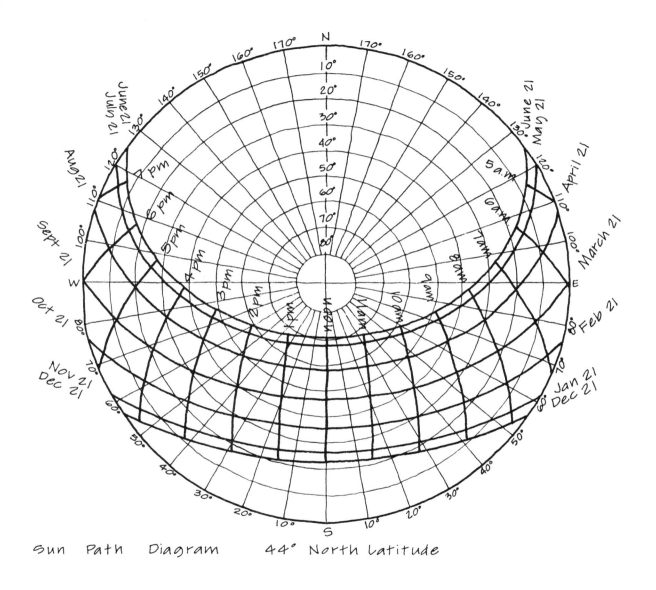

Sun Path Diagram   44° North Latitude

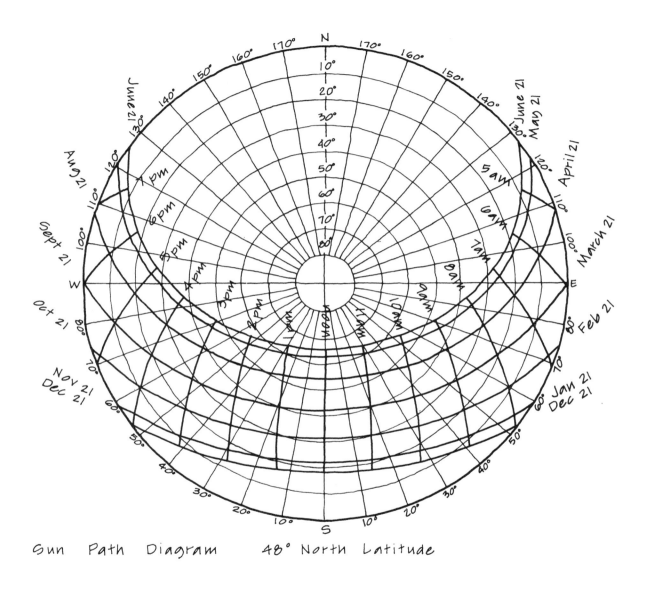

Sun Path Diagram   48° North Latitude

SUN

3. *The amount of solar radiation available each hour to offset low outside temperatures can be estimated from total daily radiation data.*

The hourly solar radiation available on a horizontal surface can be used along with the temperature, relative humidity, and wind speed on the bioclimatic chart (Technique 10) to determine the potential for human comfort at a particular time and date. Average solar radiation data for 80 cities is in Kusuda and Ishii, *Hourly Solar Radiation Data for Vertical and Horizontal Surfaces in the United States and Canada.*

If neither this nor more local sources of hourly radiation data are available, *the hourly solar radiation on a horizontal surface may be estimated as a percentage of the total daily radiation available on a horizontal surface by using the percentages in the table.* The variation within each range results from slight differences between latitudes. The table gives average daily solar radiation on a horizontal surface for four months for cities in the United States. If a city near your site is not listed, select one that has a similar latitude and climate. Remember that radiation availability can vary substantially from location to location.

Average radiation on a horizontal surface
Btu per sq. ft. per day.

City	Lat.	Jan.	Mar.	June	Sept.
Albuquerque, NM	35°	1196	2012	2756	2025
Apalachicola, FL	30°	1141	1706	2194	1644
Astoria, OR	46°	360	1076	1754	1243
Atlanta, GA	34°	873	1483	2103	1454
Bismark, ND	47°	626	1420	2178	1360
Boise, ID	44°	551	1359	2376	1622
Boston, MA	42°	534	1124	1864	1201
Brownsville, TC	26°	1125	1547	2288	1722
Charleston, SC	33°	980	1407	2111	1495
Cleveland, OH	41°	489	1275	2104	1339
Columbia, MO	30°	681	1382	2127	1603
Columbus, OH	40°	509	1170	2110	1128
Davis, CA	39°	628	1580	2618	1767
Dodge City, KS	38°	992	1637	2458	1758
East Lansing, MI	43°	449	1146	1913	1234
El Paso, TX	32°	1283	2119	2723	1998
Fort Worth, TX	33°	962	1655	2435	1808
Fresno, CA	37°	741	1730	2635	1811
Gainsville, FL	30°	1061	1684	1960	1557
Grand Junction, CO	39°	883	1706	2646	1862
Great Falls, MT	47°	562	1462	2181	1447
Greensboro, NC	36°	769	1377	2109	1447
Indianapolis, IN	40°	549	1241	2042	1437
Ithaca, NY	42°	455	1136	2026	1249
Lake Charles, LA	30°	924	1535	2208	1619
Lander, WY	43°	830	1736	2493	1619
Las Vegas, NV	36°	1074	2011	2794	1967
Lemont, IL	42°	622	1329	2041	1392
Lexington, KY	38°	274	480	673	1691
Lincoln, NB	41°	751	1376	2040	1463
Little Rock, AR	35°	726	1391	2089	1565
Los Angeles, CA	34°	961	1799	2269	1806
Madison, WI	43°	617	1304	2034	1366
Medford, OR	42°	459	1332	2440	1581
Miami, FL	26°	1318	1878	1987	1599
Nashville, TN	36°	611	1302	2146	1526

City	Lat.	Jan.	Mar.	June	Sept.
New York, NY	41°	564	1243	1995	1289
Oklahoma City, OK	35°	973	1604	2353	1739
Portland, ME	44°	593	1409	2019	1347
Rapid City, SD	44°	723	1595	2196	1538
St. Cloud, MN	46°	668	1472	2007	1288
Salt Lake City, UT	41°	650	1370	675	1602
San Antonio, TX	30°	1076	1608	2289	1778
Sault Ste. Marie, MI	46°	526	1430	2066	1131
Seattle, WA	47°	302	1056	1910	1137
Spokane, WA	48°	482	1283	2230	1419
State College, PA	41°	529	1167	2029	1268
Tampa, FL	28°	1254	1826	2142	1633
Tucson, AZ	32°	1201	515	2595	2041
Washington, DC	39°	664	1320	2078	1377

Adapted from Kusuda and Ishii.

Hour	January	March September	June
6am / 6pm	—	—	1 - 2%
7am / 5pm	—	1 - 3%	4 - 5%
8am / 4pm	0 - 4%	5 - 6%	6 - 7%
9am / 3pm	6 - 9%	8 - 9%	8 - 9%
10am / 2pm	13 - 14%	11 - 12%	10 - 11%
11am / 1pm	15 - 19%	13 - 15%	11 - 12%
12 noon	16 - 21%	14 - 15%	11 - 12%

Percentage of Total Daily Radiation on a Horizontal Surface Available Each Hour in Btu/sq. ft.

WIND

4. The direction, speed, and frequency of wind in your location can be characterized by month or year using a wind rose.

The wind rose gives detailed information about wind direction and frequency for a month or a whole year. It can be prepared with data from the *Airport Climatological Summary* (U.S. Dept. of Commerce) or other sources listed in *Index—Summarized Wind Data* (Changery, Hodge, & Ramsdell).

Using data from the table, Wind Direction vs. Wind Speed, from Table 11-A in the Airport Climatological Summary, *determine the relative frequency for each direction from the Total column. For example, the wind blows from the south 17% of the year in Eugene, Oregon. Plot this total percentage for each direction on the wind rose.*

The percentages for each wind speed group can also be plotted on the wind rose.

The annual wind rose for Eugene, Oregon, indicates that the wind comes predominantly from the north and south with the greatest frequencies in the speed group of 4 to 6 knots. Wind roses for the months of January and July for Eugene reveal that south winds occur in the winter and north winds in the summer.

Remember that the wind data from an airport site may not be exactly the same as the wind on your site. See Technique 6, air movement principles.

Wind Direct.	Wind Speed (knots)								Total	Ave. Spd.
	0-3	4-6	7-10	11-16	17-21	22-27	28-33	34-40	over 40	Total	Ave.Spd.
N	0.4	4.6	6.3	2.8	0.2	0.0				14.2	8.2
NNE	0.2	1.8	1.4	0.3	0.0					3.8	6.7
NE	0.2	1.1	0.4	0.1	0.0					1.8	5.7
ENE	0.2	0.9	0.1							1.1	4.7
E	0.2	1.0	0.1	0.0						1.4	4.7
ESE	0.3	1.4	0.8	0.1						2.6	5.8
SE	0.3	2.6	2.2	0.3						5.4	6.5
SSE	0.3	3.0	2.8	1.0	0.1	0.0	0.0			7.2	7.5
S	0.7	6.5	5.7	3.5	0.6	0.1	0.0	0.0		17.0	8.3
SSW	0.4	3.6	2.5	1.1	0.1	0.0	0.0			7.7	7.4
SW	0.4	3.1	2.7	1.1	0.1	0.0	0.0			7.4	7.3
WSW	0.3	1.8	2.1	0.7	0.1	0.0				5.0	7.4
W	0.3	1.6	1.3	0.6	0.0	0.0				3.9	7.3
WNW	0.3	1.4	0.6	0.1	0.0					2.5	6.0
NW	0.2	2.0	1.3	0.2	0.0					3.7	6.3
NNW	0.3	2.4	2.8	1.0	0.1	0.0				6.5	7.6
Calm	8.7									8.7	
Total	13.7	38.9	33.0	12.9	1.3	0.2	0.0	0.0		100.0	6.7

Table 11-A Wind Direction vs. Wind Speed Eugene Annual

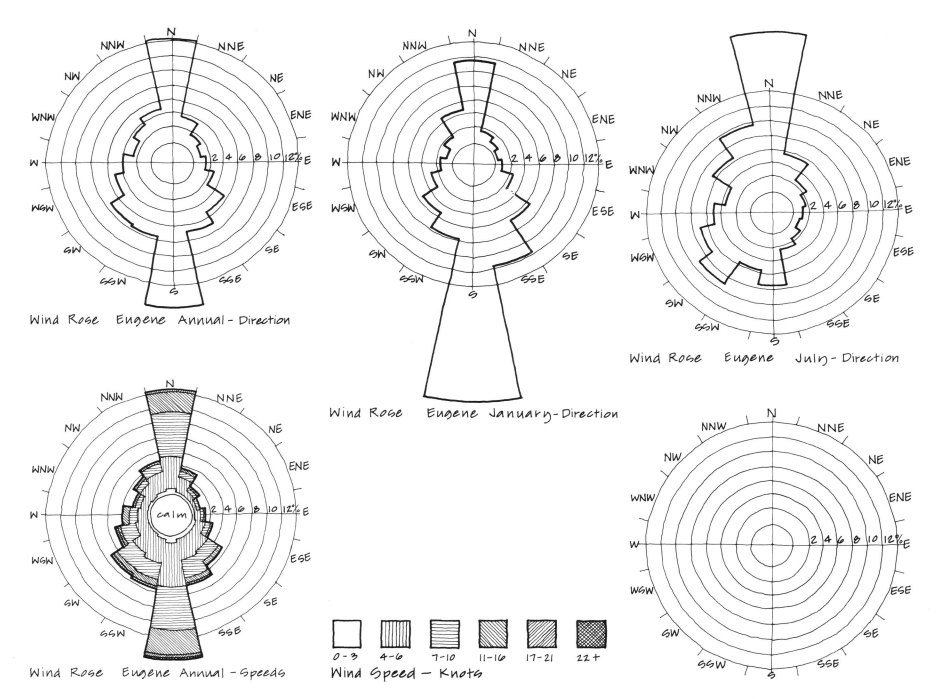

Wind Rose   Eugene   Annual - Direction

Wind Rose   Eugene   January - Direction

Wind Rose   Eugene   July - Direction

Wind Rose   Eugene   Annual - Speeds

0-3	4-6	7-10	11-16	17-21	22+

Wind Speed — Knots

WIND

5. ***Wind direction and speed by time of day and month of the year can be determined for your location using a wind square.***

The wind square gives more time-specific information than the wind rose does. It tabulates, for three-hour periods and for each month, the predominant wind speed, the predominant wind direction at that speed, and the percentage of time that the wind blows from that direction.

Several conclusions can be drawn from the wind square. Because it is organized by month and time it can be used in conjunction with the bioclimatic chart to anticipate the speed and direction of the wind when the temperature and humidity are above or below the comfort zone.

From the New York City wind square (based on Loftness, Ch. 12), one can determine that the wind comes from the northwest during the winter and from the south in the summer, so there is little conflict on the site between blocking the chilling winter winds and admitting the ventilating summer winds. Also, wind speed is greatest during the daytime and lowest at night.

Wind data are collected by several organizations in varying formats, and breakdowns by time, speed, direction, and month are frequently limited. Data available by state and city are listed in *Index—Summarized Wind Data,* by Changery et al. The *Airport Climatological Summary* published by the National Oceanic and Atmospheric Administration (NOAA) (U.S. Dept. of Commerce) lists wind data for 130 major airports.

To make a wind square using the data from Airport Climatological Summary, *find the month of the year you want to study in Table*

2, *Weather Condition by Hour—Mean Number of Days. This table lists wind speed by speed group (1–6 knots, 7–10 knots, etc.) and time of day in three-hour intervals. For each combination of wind speed and time, the table presents the number of days in which that wind speed was measured. Select the highest frequency for each three-hour period and assign that wind speed to the appropriate cell in the wind square.*

Next, use this wind speed group to enter Table 1, Wind Direction vs. Wind Speed. Move down the column headed by this wind speed. Identify the highest percentage of observations to select the direction from which the wind is blowing. This is the predominant wind direction at that wind speed for the hour group under consideration.

You may wish to draw the length of the wind direction arrow in the wind square in proportion to the percentage of time the wind blows from the predominant direction. Simply divide the percentage of observations for a particular direction by the total percentage of observations for all directions in that speed group found in the bottom row of Table 1 (Loftness, p. 39).

For example, for the month of January in Eugene, Table 2 indicates that hour group 01–03 has the highest number of occurrences, 12.7, in the wind speed group 1–6 knots. Therefore 1–6 knots would be assigned to the cell in the wind square corresponding to the first hour group and the first month. Using the 1–6 knots speed group, Table 1 indicates that the greatest number of observations (7.6 = 7.0 + .6) is for wind blowing from the south. They account for 21% of the observations in this time period [21% = 7.6 ÷ (32.5 + 13.6 − 9.8)]. (Calm periods are excluded from calculations.) Therefore, the wind direction arrow length should be proportional to 21%. The

Wind Square   New York City

completed wind square shows the 21% wind arrow pointing the direction of wind movement. The field of the square is white, indicating the 1–6 knot wind speed group.

It is important to keep in mind that wind data are usually collected at airports and that the wind speed and direction on your site may be quite different (Robinette, 1972, p. 73; Air Movement Principles, Technique 6).

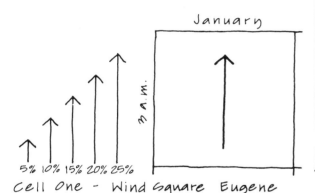

Cell One – Wind Square   Eugene

Wind Direct.	Wind Speed (knots)									Total	Ave. Spd.
	0-3	4-6	7-10	11-16	17-21	22-27	28-33	34-40	over 40		
N	0.6	4.7	4.1	1.8	0.3					11.4	7.6
NNE	0.3	0.9	0.4							1.6	5.2
NE	0.1	0.7	0.2							1.0	5.0
ENE	0.2	0.4								0.5	4.2
E	0.1	0.6	0.1							0.8	4.9
ESE		1.3	1.1	0.2						2.6	7.0
SE	0.0	2.4	3.5	0.5						6.4	7.3
SSE	0.4	3.1	5.4	2.7	0.2					11.7	8.5
S	0.6	7.0	10.8	9.6	1.7	0.4				30.1	9.9
SSW	0.3	2.8	2.9	1.3	0.2	0.0				7.5	8.0
SW	0.4	2.5	1.1	0.8	0.1		0.0			5.0	7.3
WSW	0.2	1.4	0.8	0.4	0.0					2.7	6.9
W	0.2	0.8	0.3	0.1	0.0					1.5	6.1
WNW	0.1	0.7	0.1		0.0					0.9	5.9
NW	0.2	1.4	0.2							1.8	5.0
NNW	0.2	1.9	1.6	0.7	0.1					4.6	7.5
Calm	9.8									9.8	
Total	13.6	32.5	32.8	18.0	2.6	0.5	0.0			100.0	7.4

Table 1 Wind Direction vs. Wind Speed   Eugene January

Weather Conditions	Hour							
	01	04	07	10	13	16	19	22
Calm	3.4	4.4	3.7	2.7	1.6	2.3	3.3	3.0
1-6	12.7	11.5	11.1	10.3	9.1	10.5	12.7	11.9
7-10	9.3	9.4	10.8	10.9	10.5	9.5	10.1	10.8
11-16	4.6	4.9	4.5	6.4	7.8	7.7	4.3	4.5
17-21	0.8	0.7	0.7	0.4	1.7	0.9	0.5	0.8
22-27	0.1	0.1	0.2	0.3	0.3	0.1	0.1	
28-33	0.1							
over 33								

(Wind Speed (knots))

Table 2 Weather Conditions by Hour   Eugene January

WIND

6. *Airport wind data can be adjusted to approximate wind flow on your site using air movement principles.*

The information in wind squares and wind roses, Techniques 5 and 4, frequently comes from an airport, which may have wind flow patterns quite different than those of nearby sites.

The wind flow patterns for a particular site can be understood in relation to airport data by simulating the way the site modifies the wind in a wind tunnel (Aynsley, Melbourne, & Vickery, p. 71). When wind tunnel tests aren't feasible, the designer can estimate wind direction and speed by using three principles that govern air movement and by becoming familiar with the way wind interacts with natural and built forms.

The first of the three principles is that, as a result of friction, air velocity is slower near the surface of the earth than higher in the atmosphere. The reduction in velocity is a function of the ground's roughness, so the wind velocity profiles are quite different for different terrain types (Melaragno, p. 45). The diagrams show, for the three terrain types, the height at which the gradient velocity is reached. Wind velocities measured at a site near the ground are frequently lower than those measured at the airport towers and presented in most climatological data. Likewise, exposed sites or buildings at altitudes higher than the airport tower are likely to experience higher velocities. Assuming that the airport wind velocities were measured at 30 feet above the ground, you can use the curves to approximate the adjusted velocity for any height and any terrain.

The second principle is that, as a result of inertia, air tends to continue moving the same direction when it meets an obstruction. There-

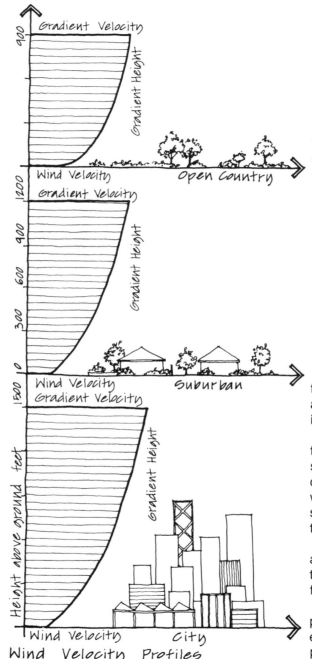

Wind Velocity Profiles

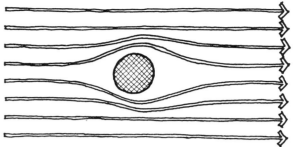

Wind Flow Around an Object

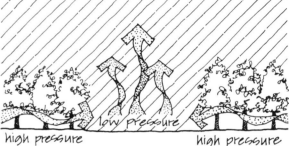

Wind Flow from High to Low Pressure Zones

fore, it flows around objects, like water flows around a rock in a stream, rather than bouncing off the object in random directions.

Third, air flows from areas of high pressure to areas of low pressure. For example, when solar radiation heats the air in a meadow, reducing its pressure and causing it to rise, air will then flow into the meadow area from the surrounding forest, where the air is at a relatively lower temperature and higher pressure.

Using these principles and realizing that air acts like a fluid, like water, it is often possible to visualize how windflow on a site might differ from windflow at a nearby airport.

In addition to these air movement principles, there are several microclimate phenomena that often occur on building sites (Olgyay, pp. 45, 94; Robinette, 1972, p. 73).

Near bodies of water, the breeze blows off the water toward the land during the day. The land heats up more rapidly than the water, causing the air over the land to rise and be replaced by the air from over the water. At night the flow is reversed, with the breeze blowing from the land, which has cooled more rapidly than the water, to the water, which is relatively warmer than the land, as the air over it rises and is replaced by the cooler air from over the land.

In valleys, the wind blows uphill during the day because the sun warms the air, causing it to rise. At night the air flow reverses because cold ground surfaces cool the surrounding air, making it heavier and causing it to flow down the valley. The phenomenon of cool air falling also results in cool air flowing down hills at night and collecting in pockets formed by topography or vegetation.

When wind meets an object like a building or a hill, it creates a high pressure zone of reduced velocity on the windward side of the object (the side the wind is blowing toward) and a low pressure zone of low velocity on the leeward side of the object. The velocity is increased as the wind sweeps around the sides and over the top of the object.

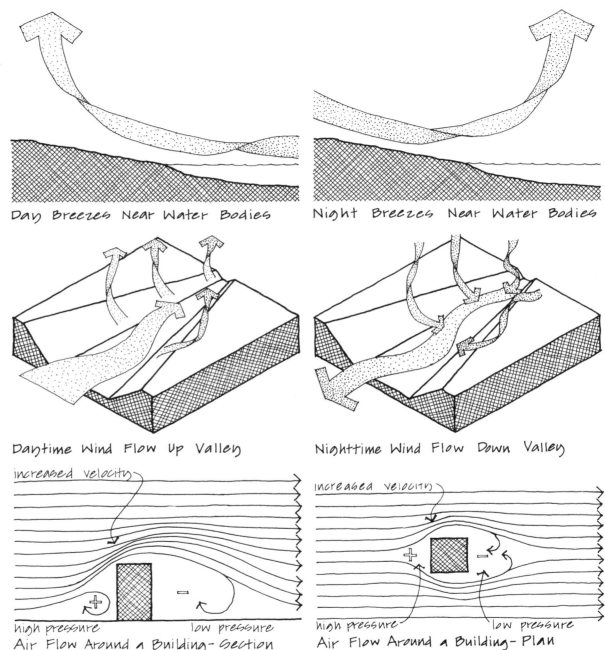

Day Breezes Near Water Bodies

Night Breezes Near Water Bodies

Daytime Wind Flow Up Valley

Nighttime Wind Flow Down Valley

increased velocity

high pressure   low pressure
Air Flow Around a Building - Section

increased velocity

high pressure   low pressure
Air Flow Around a Building - Plan

SUN AND WIND

7. *The most favorable building locations on a site can be determined by analyzing the combined availability of sun and wind.*

The thermal comfort zone shown on the bioclimatic chart, Technique 10, may be expanded by admitting or blocking the wind and sun at appropriate temperature and relative humidity levels. The permutations of admitting and blocking sun and wind are represented in the microclimate matrix (Brown, 1982, pp. 3-12). As an example, Condition C, Admit Sun-Block Wind, is a response that would be appropriate for an exterior space if the temperature were below the standard comfort zone. Throughout the year all four matrix conditions may occur at various locations on a site as a result of sun position, wind direction, site topography, vegetation, and existing buildings. They may create more or less favorable building sites, depending on the climate conditions with which they coincide.

This matrix can be used before any buildings are proposed to see where favorable sites exist and after buildings are proposed to see what microclimates are created around the buildings.

Select time periods to be analyzed from the bioclimatic chart, Technique 10. The following example is from *Inside Out* (Brown, Reynolds, & Ubbelohde, Ch. 3). For Salem, Oregon, the hottest and coldest months, July and January, are both analyzed at 12 noon. The July average conditions call for admitting the wind and blocking the sun for the middle part of the day. The January average conditions call for admitting the sun and blocking the wind all day.

Using information from the wind square or wind rose, Techniques 5 or 4, and the wind flow principles, Technique 6, estimate how the wind might flow over the site. In Salem, the wind blows from the south in the winter and from the northwest in the summer. When the wind blows from the south, it will create areas of reduced velocity on the north side of the ridge and on the north and south sides of the trees, and areas of increased velocity to the east and west of the trees (Olgyay, p. 99; Robinette, 1972, p. 72). When the wind blows from the northwest, it will create an area of reduced velocity southeast of the trees and may reduce velocity on the north side of the ridge.

Use the sundial, Technique 1, and a model to plot the shaded areas of the site for the time periods under consideration. In Salem in January, the ridge casts shadows on the site at 10 AM and noon but not at 2 PM. In July, the ridge shades only a small part of the site at 10 AM and creates no shadows at noon or 2 PM.

Now combine the wind flow and the shadows for January at noon and label each part of the site in terms of the matrix categories A, B, C, and D. It is now clear that Condition C, Admit Sun–Block Wind, which is appropriate for Salem's January climate, occurs only just south of the trees. (Note that it will probably also occur on the south side of a building placed in a sunny area.) Areas marked B or D are probably not appropriate locations for a solar-heated building since they are frequently in shade, but areas marked A or C probably have sufficient access to the sun.

The diagram that combines wind flow and shadow plots for noon in July reveals that there aren't any areas on the site that produce the desired Condition B, Admit Wind–Block Sun, because the existing site provides no shaded areas. An appropriate strategy in this case would be to select an area of the site that has wind, an A or B area, and then create shade with vegetation or a building.

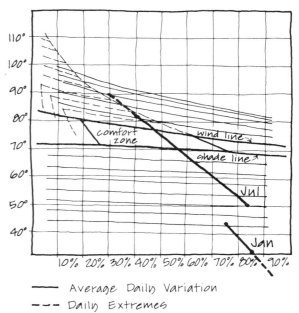

	Admit Sun	Block Sun
Admit Wind	A	B
Block Wind	C	D

Microclimate Matrix

—— Average Daily Variation
‐ ‐ ‐ Daily Extremes

Salem, Oregon Jan/Jul Average/Extreme

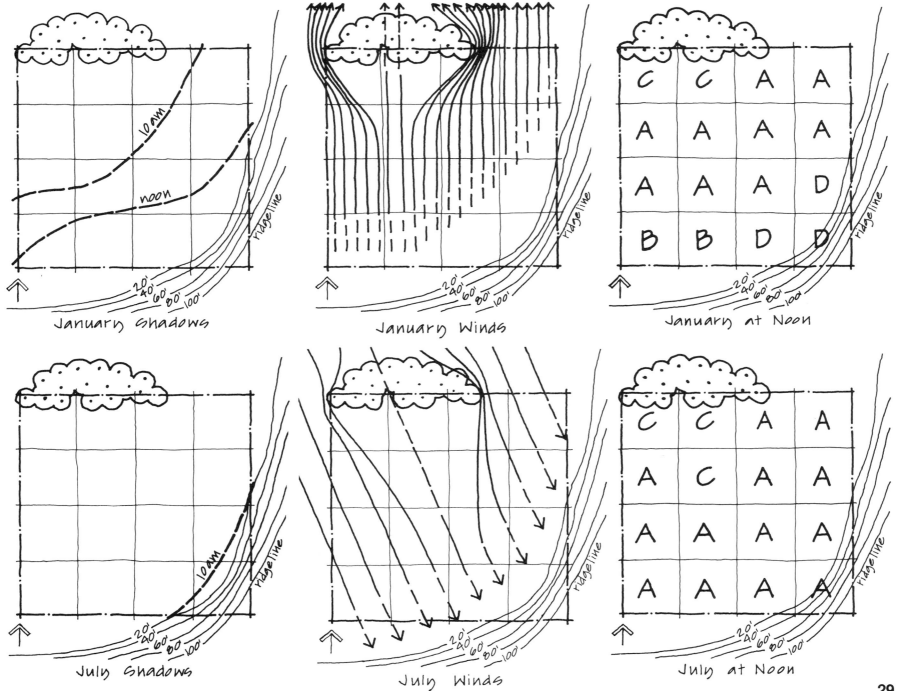

January Shadows

January Winds

January at Noon

July Shadows

July Winds

July at Noon

29

LIGHT

8. *Daylighting design conditions can be determined by plotting skycover.*

For daylighting purposes, sky conditions are classified as either overcast, clear, or partly cloudy. Each classification has characteristics that influence daylighting design. (For a more extensive discussion, see Hopkinson, Petherbridge, & Longmore, pp. 29-58, and B. Evans, pp. 95-105.) The overcast sky is defined as one in which the position of the sun cannot be determined due to density of cloud cover; the light is diffuse and relatively even over the sky dome. The overcast sky is three times brighter at the zenith than at the horizon, and the illumination is evenly distributed around the zenith. Therefore, the top of the sky dome is the source of the most illumination. The overcast sky is frequently used as the minimum design condition, though the actual amount of illumination can vary from a few hundred to several thousand footcandles, depending on the altitude of the sun and the density of the cloud cover.

Illumination from the sun's direct rays is extremely powerful compared to that reflected from the sky dome; however, not including the sun, the clear sky is less bright than the overcast sky. The distribution of light from a clear sky, with the exception of the sun and the area immediately around it, is opposite that of the overcast sky—three times brighter at the horizon than at the zenith. Therefore, building openings that face the top of the sky dome, do not face reflective surfaces, and do not admit direct light may receive less light on clear days than on overcast days.

The illumination from a clear sky varies with the position of the sun, the season, and the amount of water vapor in the atmosphere. Therefore, the amount of illumination avail-

able to any surface will change throughout the day and year and may vary considerably depending on local conditions.

Sunlight reflected from the ground usually represents 10 to 15% of the total illumination reaching a vertical window, though it can account for more than 50% when the window is shaded from direct radiation. Reflected light from the ground can be a good source of daylighting during clear sky conditions because it reflects again off the usually lighter ceiling and penetrates deeply into the room. Because direct sunlight is so powerful, it is a potential source of glare and may introduce an undesirable source of heat gain.

The third classification, the partly cloudy sky, describes the most common condition. Days that are either uniformly overcast or perfectly clear are the exception in most regions of the United States. Most skies are partly cloudy and fall somewhere between the extremes of overcast skies that have a few clear spots and mostly clear skies that have a few clouds. Overcast skies with bright spots take on some of the character of clear skies; that illumination levels depend on sun position. Clear skies with clouds are frequently very bright if both direct sunlight and light reflected from clouds are available at the same time. Partly cloudy skies frequently exhibit very different amounts of illumination across the sky dome as the cloud cover changes over time. As a result, estimation procedures must be regarded as preliminary approximations. (For more information on illumination levels, see Illuminating Engineering Society [IES], *Recommended Practice of Daylighting*, p. 23).

Daylighting conditions for your climate can be estimated by plotting the average number of clear, cloudly, and partly cloudy days as a percentage of the total days in the month.

Overcast Sky

Partly Cloudy Sky

zenith

horizon

Clear Sky

Use either the monthly totals from *Local Climatological Data: Annual Summary with Comparative Data* or *Comparative Climate Data Through 1976* (U.S. Dept. of Commerce) for a location near your site.

To illustrate, Salem, Oregon, has about the same number of partly cloudy days throughout the year, but the number of clear and overcast days changes dramatically from winter to summer. The overcast condition predominates and is a primary concern in daylighting design, though the clear and partly cloudy conditions must also be accommodated.

Illumination resulting from a variety of cloud conditions can be approximated from the graph. *Determine the solar altitude from a sun path diagram for the hour and month in question. Enter the chart at the altitude, move vertically to the appropriate curve, and then horizontally to read illumination in footcandles.*

A more detailed ananlysis of sky cover can be prepared with a sky cover square that relates varying sky cover to time of day and month of the year. Three-hour interval sky-cover data can be found for most air force bases in *Revised Uniform Summary of Surface Weather Observations* (Loftness, p. 41).

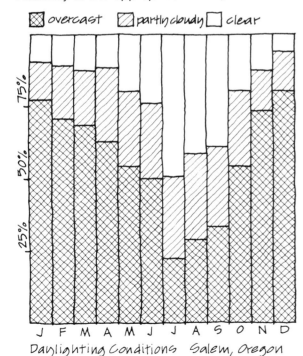

Daylighting Conditions Salem, Oregon

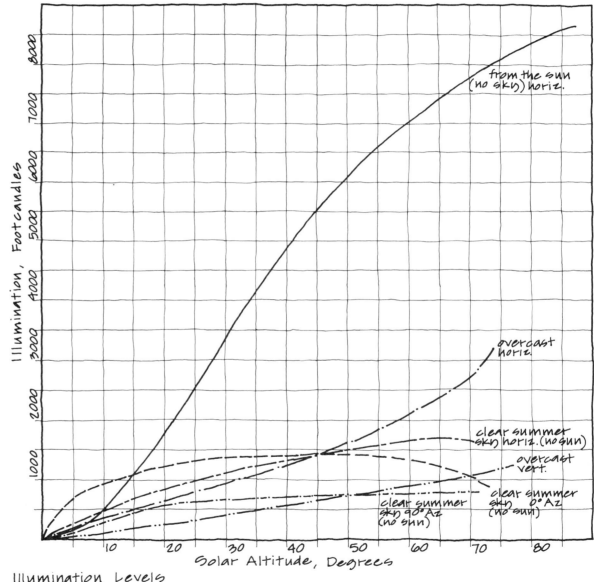

Illumination Levels

LIGHT

9. *Daylight availability curves can be used to determine the percentage of time a desired level of illumination can be achieved in your location.*

The percentage of exterior illumination available inside the building is called the "daylight factor." It is a function of window size and placement, sky obstructions, glazing transmission, and interior reflectances (Strategy 59). The total amount of exterior illumination available is a function of weather conditions and latitude (Technique 8). If a certain percentage of the total exterior illumination is assumed to be available inside the building, usually 1 to 10%, then daylight availability curves can be used to determine the percentage of time that illumination level will be available for a given latitude and set of working hours (Commission Internationale de l'Eclairage [CIE], p. 5).

Enter the chart at the latitude of your site and move down until the horizontal line corresponding to the desired average interior illumination is intersected. Curves A through F correspond to the percentage of time the desired illumination levels will be met or exceeded for a given time interval. Time intervals and curve percentages can be determined from the table.

The daylight availability curves are based on average weather conditions for typical climates; therefore, some years will have more or less light than the average condition, and some dry climates will have higher illumination levels.

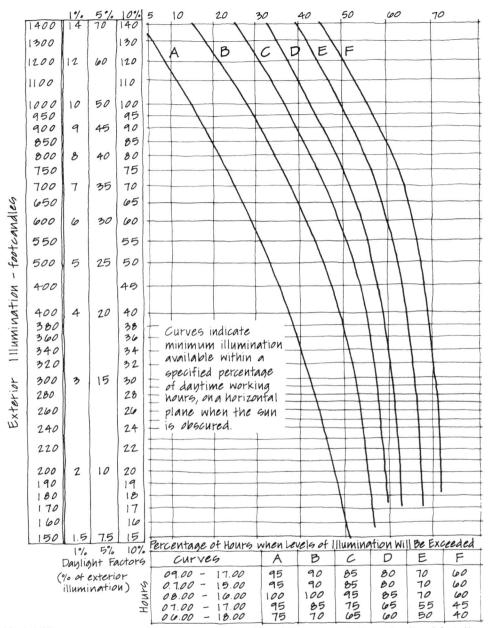

Curves indicate minimum illumination available within a specified percentage of daytime working hours, on a horizontal plane when the sun is obscured.

Daylight Availability

Percentage of Hours when Levels of Illumination Will Be Exceeded						
Curves	A	B	C	D	E	F
09.00 - 17.00	95	90	85	80	70	60
07.00 - 15.00	95	90	85	80	70	60
08.00 - 16.00	100	100	95	85	70	60
07.00 - 17.00	95	85	75	65	55	45
06.00 - 18.00	75	70	65	60	50	40

adapted from: 'Daylight: International Recommendations for the Calculation of Natural Daylight', Internation Commission on Illumination CIE No 16 (E-3.2) 1970

COMFORT

10. *Architectural responses that produce thermal comfort in your climate can be determined by using the bioclimatic chart.*

The bioclimatic chart shows the relationship of the four major climate variables that determine human comfort (Arens et al., p. 1202; Olgyay, p. 19). By plotting temperature and relative humidity, you can determine if the resulting condition is comfortable (within the comfort zone), too hot (above the top of the comfort zone), or too cold (below the bottom of the comfort zone). The chart shown, based on work by Arens et al., assumes a 0.8 clo level, which is typical for winter clothing, and an activity level of 1.3 Met, equivalent to slow walking or office work. Furthermore, if the temperature–humidity combination falls above the shading line, then shading is assumed. If the temperature–humidity combination is below the wind line, still air is assumed.

Point A corresponds to a temperature of 48°F and a relative humidity of 52%, a condition usually described as too cold for comfort. Because point A is below the wind line, it is assumed that the wind is blocked. If the wind were not blocked, the condition would feel even colder due to the chilling effect of the wind.

The horizontal lines below the shading line indicate increments of solar radiation falling on a horizontal surface that can compensate for successively lower ambient air temperatures. At point A, if there were approximately 130 Btu per hr. per sq. ft. of solar radiation available, this would provide enough warmth to offset the low temperature, and a person would feel comfortable if there were no air movement.

At point B, with a temperature of 80°F and 70% relative humidity, if a person were in the shade and a wind of 2.2 miles per hour (mph) were available, the cooling effect of the wind would produce comfort.

At point C, with a temperature of 92°F and 15% relative humidity, conditions can be made comfortable by evaporating water into the air, thereby cooling it. The dotted lines indicate the amount of evaporation required per pound of dry air.

One of the most useful ways of analyzing a climate is to plot an average day for each month of the year on the bioclimatic chart. Temperature and humidity can be plotted hourly, in three-hour intervals, or in twelve-hour intervals. Because average maximum and minimum temperatures and humidities are easily available for many locations, twelve-hour intervals are usually the simplest to plot. A good source of information, usually in the local library, is the *Local Climatological Data, Annual Summary with Comparative Data,* for your location, published by the National Oceanic and Atmospheric Administration (NOAA), National Climatic Center, Asheville, North Carolina (U.S. Dept. of Commerce).

When using the average maximum and minimum, plot the maximum temperature with the minimum relative humidity and the minimum temperature with the maximum relative humidity. Draw a line connecting these two points. This line approximates the change in temperature and humidity over the day. By assuming that the high temperature occurs at 4 PM and the low temperature occurs at 4 AM, the line may be subdivided into equal increments that can be used to approximate the temperature and relative humidity at any time of the day.

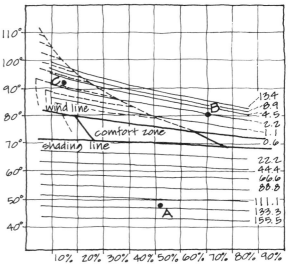

Bioclimatic Chart

Remember that this is only an approximation—the highs and lows do not occur at twelve-hour intervals in all seasons, and temperature does not change at a constant rate (Loftness, p. 13; Watson & Glover, p. 35).

Several types of information can be gathered from a plot of twelve months. For example, the bioclimatic chart for Phoenix indicates that while the climate is cold in the winter, it rarely gets below the point that can be offset by solar radiation. The amount of solar radiation available can be approximated by the methods outlined in Technique 3. The temperature–humidity lines for each day are long and fairly steeply inclined, indicating large daily temperature swings. This indicates that heating and cooling techniques that store heat or cold from one time of the day to use in another may be effective. Evaporation alone will work as a cooling strategy in the months of May and June. To a limited extent, wind can be used to cool. The availability of wind can be estimated from the wind square analysis, Technique 5.

It is important to realize that these plots represent outdoor conditions. A building changes its internal microclimate by virtue of the thermal lag of its materials, its controlled infiltration rate, etc. This is especially true of large buildings, which generate a lot of internal heat and are therefore less affected by climate than smaller buildings. See Techniques 18 and 19.

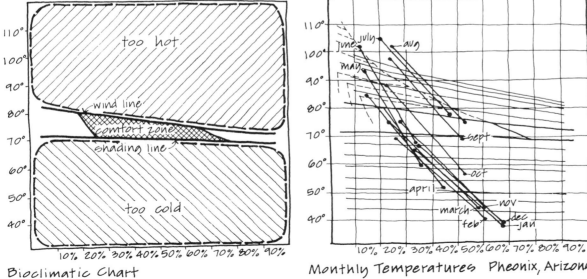

Bioclimatic Chart

Monthly Temperatures Pheonix, Arizona

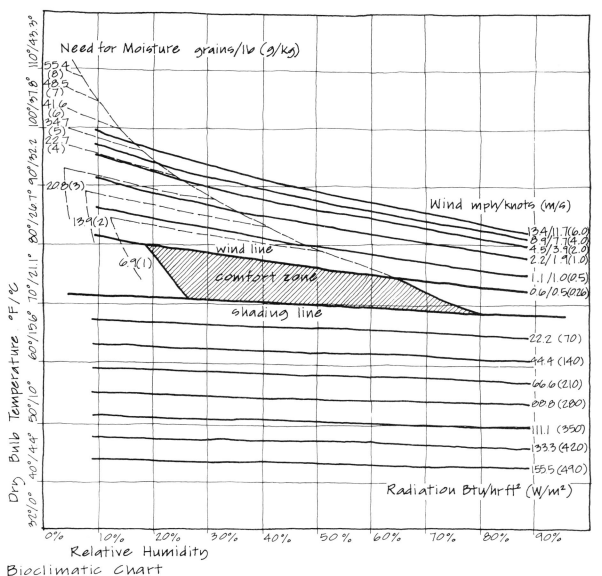

Bioclimatic Chart

B

Program and Use

Knowing how and when a building is used is critical in determining the building's heating and cooling requirements. Buildings that have low levels of use generate little internal heat, and their heating and cooling needs depend on the climate's characteristics. If the climate is cold, buildings need heating; if it's warm, they need cooling. Buildings that have high levels of use may generate so much internal heat that no matter how cold it gets, they still need cooling. In most buildings, the rate and timing of internal heat generation is closely linked to occupancy. People give off heat, which is especially important when they are densely packed. But more importantly, when people enter a building, they turn on its lights and equipment, both of which are sources of heat in the space. Obviously there are buildings in which equipment runs without many people, like computing centers or automated factories, but these are the exceptions, not the rule.

Because the internal heat gain is normally so closely linked to how people use the building, the rate of gain changes over the day and week. For example, an office building may experience its greatest gain in the morning and the afternoon, with a reduction at noon when people leave for lunch and a larger reduction at night and on weekends. Apartment buildings might experience quite a different pattern, generating heat in the early evening and on weekends. However, this gain is probably at a lesser rate than in an office building because there are fewer people and lights and less equipment per unit of floor area.

Cooling requirements for a building are frequently accentuated when the timing of internal heat gain coincides with heat gain from the climate. This is often the case in office buildings that experience intense use in the afternoon, coinciding in warm climates with the maximum outside temperatures and intense radiation on vertical west-facing surfaces. This occurs frequently in some areas, so that utility companies that supply electricity to those areas experience their peak loads in the afternoon. Design strategies that can reduce cooling loads during these peak periods not only reduce the building's need for energy, but also help reduce the area's need to build more electricity-generating capacity.

The analysis techniques in this section are divided into three groups: Occupancy, Electric Lighting, and Equipment. They are directed primarily at supplying information for Heating and Cooling Patterns, Techniques 18 and 19, and should be used in conjunction with them. However, because they reveal the most important major sources of internal heat generation, they can suggest design strategies to reduce these gains. For example, daylighting reduces the electric-lighting load and is usually available in the afternoon when the electric utility may be reaching its peak. Rates of heat gain from people, equipment, and lights are listed by building type in Heating and Cooling Patterns, Technique 18.

OCCUPANCY

11. *Estimate the internal heat gain from building occupants to understand their contribution to the building's heating and cooling requirements.*

The metabolic energy of people can contribute substantially to the amount of heat generated in the building. This heat may increase the cooling requirement in a hot climate or in a building that has a cooling load due to other internal sources of heat gain, or it may decrease the heating requirements of a building in a cool climate.

The amount of heat and moisture generated by people is a function of sex, age, activity, and other factors. Most passive cooling systems cannot remove water vapor from the air; therefore, only the sensible heat (that which raises the air temperature) gains are considered in determining the internal heat gains from people. Conventional mechanical refrigeration systems that remove moisture from the air in the cooling process require additional energy to condense the water vapor, to prevent an uncomfortable increase in humidity at the lower temperature. This additional load on the cooling system is called "latent heat" (McGuinness, Stein, & Reynolds, p. 228) and should be added to the sensible heat gain to determine the total heat gain for systems that remove water vapor in addition to cooling the air.

The total sensible heat gain from people, in Btu's, is found by multiplying the occupancy of the building by the rate of heat gain per person (ASHRAE, 1972, p. 416). The occupancy of a building may be determined for either peak or average conditions. The peak condition indicates the maximum requirements of the systems, frequently a passive plus back-

Degree of Activity	Sensible Heat Gain Btu/hr	Latent Heat Gain Btu/hr
seated at rest, seated light work	225 to 245	105 to 155
moderately active office work, walking slowly	250	200 to 250
light bench work, moderate dancing	275 to 300	475 to 545
walking fast, moderately heavy work	375	625
heavy work, bowling	580	870

Rate of Heat Gain from People

up system; the average occupancy indicates the capacity of the systems under normal conditions.

To determine the rate of internal gain, first locate on the horizontal axis the number of people per 100 sq. ft. of occupied area. Then move vertically to the diagonal line corresponding to the people's activity level. Next move horizontally to the vertical axis, which indicates the rate of internal gain from people in Btu per hr. per sq. ft. of floor area.

Different occupancies for different parts of the building and different activity levels can be done separately and then summed.

Heat gain from people, lights, and equipment by building type is listed in Technique 18.

assembly areas - concentrated use, auditoriums, churches, dance floors	14
assembly areas - less concentrated use, conference rooms, dining rooms, exhibit rooms, gyms, lounges	7
classrooms	5
retail stores - ground floor	3
dormitories, library reading rooms, locker rooms, daycare	2
offices	1
hotels, apartments, commercial kitchens	.5
warehouses, dwellings	.3

People per 100 sq. ft. of Occupied Area For estimating Peak Conditions

adapted from: <u>Uniform Building Code</u>, International Conference of Building Officials, 1979

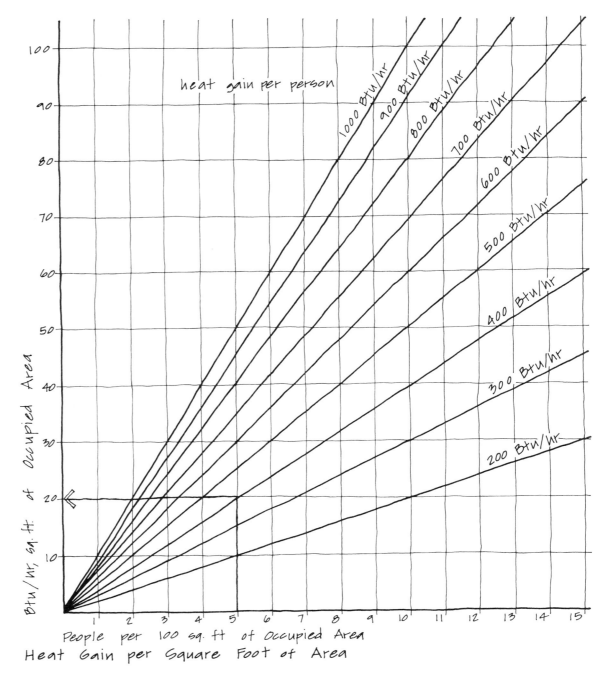

heat gain per person

Heat Gain per Square Foot of Area

ELECTRIC LIGHTING

12. *Estimate the internal heat gain from electric lighting to understand its contribution to the building's heating and cooling requirements.*

Electric lighting contributes heat to occupied spaces as an inevitable by-product of its function as illumination. Unless special heat-removal techniques are used, almost all of the electrical power fed into the lights eventually generates heat in the occupied space. The amount of heat generated from lights is a function of the illumination level and the efficiency of the light source. To the degree that daylighting is used to meet the desired illumination level, electric-lighting levels may be reduced.

To determine the heat gain from lights, assuming no daylighting contribution, *first select the footcandle level appropriate for your building or space* (B. Evans, p. 18). *Find this level on the vertical axis of the graph, then move horizontally until you intersect the diagonal line representing the lighting type to be used. Finally, drop a vertical line to the horizontal axis and read the heat gain in Btu per hr. per sq. ft. of building floor area.*

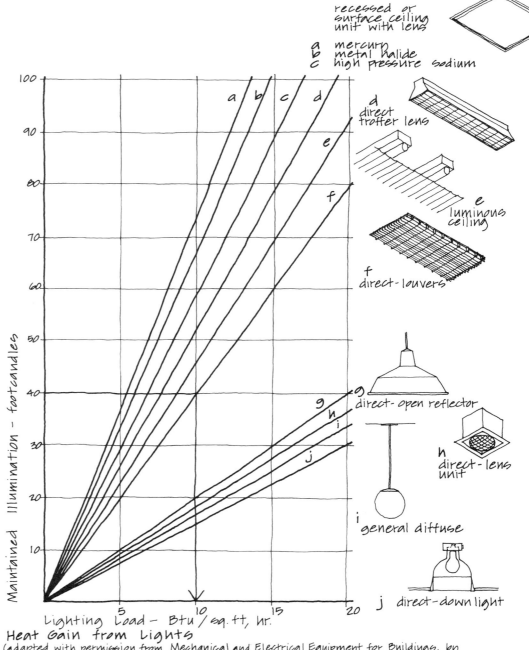

a mercury
b metal halide
c high pressure sodium

d direct troffer lens

e luminous ceiling

f direct-louvers

g direct-open reflector

h direct-lens unit

i general diffuse

j direct-down light

recessed or surface ceiling unit with lens

Maintained Illumination - footcandles

Lighting Load — Btu / sq. ft, hr.

Heat Gain from Lights
(adapted with permission from Mechanical and Electrical Equipment for Buildings, by McGuinness, Stein and Reynolds, 6th edition, 1980, p. 867)

Type of Activity	Illuminance-fc		
	low	mean	high
General Lighting			
public spaces - dark surroundings	2	3	5
simple orientation for short stay	5	7.5	10
working spaces - occasional visual task	10	15	20
visual task - high contrast or large size	20	30	50
Illumination on Task			
visual task - medium contrast or small size	50	75	100
visual task - low contrast or very small size	100	150	200

Illumination Levels

EQUIPMENT

13. *Estimate the internal heat gain from equipment in the building to understand its contribution to the building's heating and cooling requirements.*

Electrical equipment and appliances operating in a space contribute heat to that space as a by-product of their operation. The amount of heat generated is a function of the kind of equipment used, the amount of equipment, and how often it is operated. *Typical equipment heat gains for some building types are given in the table.* When the exact equipment is known, its heat contribution may be estimated from the tables in ASHRAE *Handbook of Fundamentals,* 1972, pp. 417–419. These estimates are especially useful for special building types, such as laboratories and factories, or for areas within buildings, such as kitchens, with a high concentration of equipment.

Heat gain from equipment, lights, and people by building type is listed in Combining Climate, Program, and Form, Technique 18.

	Btu/hr, sq ft
general office	3–4
purchasing & accounting office	6–7
office w/ computer display	15
office w/ digital computers	75–175
office w/ analog computers	50–150
laboratory	15–70
plant – general assembly	20
plant – curing processes	150
residential – single family	2–3
residential – multi family	2–3
retail store	3–4
library	3–4
school	3–4
theater / auditorium	1–2
sports arena	1–2

Heat Gain from Equipment

C

Form and Envelope

Heat gain from electric lights, people, and equipment by building type is listed in Combining Climate, Program, and Form, Technique 18.

The building itself is the third basic factor that influences the heating and cooling requirements. Its shape and construction greatly influence how much of the climate and internal loads are actually translated into heating or cooling requirements. For example, a building located in a sunny hot climate experiences a tremendous load from the sun per square foot of surface. However, if the building is shaped and oriented so as to reduce the area exposed to the sun, the glazing is shaded, and the walls are insulated, much of that solar load can be prevented from increasing the cooling requirements.

Like the techniques in Program and Use, these techniques are primarily directed at supplying information to Heating and Cooling Patterns (Technique 19) and probably will be used most often in conjunction with them. Technique 14 under Heat Flow through the Envelope estimates how fast the heat will flow through the building's skin for each 1°F difference between inside and outside temperatures. The designer can understand how the ratio of skin area to floor area, percentage of window area, and wall construction affect the rate of heat flow. Because this rate of heat flow depends on a temperature difference, it is not important for some passive systems like natural ventilation, which do not depend on creating a difference in temperature between inside and out. The rate of heat flow is also related to occupancy because the inside temperature is determined by human comfort criteria. When the building isn't occupied, the inside temperature can be allowed to float at or nearer to the outside temperature, thereby reducing the temperature difference between inside and out and the magnitude of heat flow.

Technique 16, Ventilation and Infiltration Heat Loss and Gain, is related to both occupancy and envelope construction. When outside air enters the building it must be either heated or cooled if a difference in temperature is being maintained between inside and out. Air that leaks in (infiltration) is not related to occupancy but the amount of ventilation air required is, and therefore heating or cooling can be greatly reduced when the building isn't occupied.

Heat gain from the sun, analyzed with Technique 15, is very dependent on the building's form, orientation, and amount of glazing, as well as the climate, which determines the sun's availability. Estimating solar impact is somewhat time-consuming and, if the glazing area is very small or if the climatic and internal gains are such that conditions are only accentuated, not changed, then heat gain through glazing may be omitted. The technique will demonstrate to the designer the degree of importance of the amount of glazing, its orientation, and its shading in heat gain.

Skin and ventilation loss and gain and solar gain can be estimated by building type from the tables in Heating and Cooling Patterns, Technique 18.

HEAT FLOW THROUGH THE ENVELOPE

14. *Estimate the rate of heat flow through the skin to understand its contribution to the building's heating and cooling requirements.*

The amount of heat that flows through a building's skin due to a temperature difference between inside and outside is a function of the magnitude of that difference, the resistance to heat flow by the skin materials, and area of the skin. Because heat flows from hot to cold, if the inside is warmer than the outside, the heat will flow outward. If the inside is cooler than the outside, the heat will flow inward.

The rate of heat flow through building materials is usually described in terms of resistance (R). R is the number of hours needed for 1 Btu to flow through one square foot of skin given a temperature difference of 1°F. The reciprocal of R, the U-value, is the number of Btu's that will flow through one square foot of building skin in one hour given a temperature difference of 1°F (McGuinness et al., p. 103).

Glass has a much lower resistance to heat flow than other building materials. For example, single glazing has a U-value of 1.13 Btu per hr. F° per sq. ft. (R = .88), while an uninsulated wood stud wall has a U-value of 0.24 Btu per hr. F° per sq. ft. (R = 4.17). The resistance of opaque walls increases dramatically as insulation is added to the wall, at a rate of approximately R = 4 per inch of insulation. Therefore, the amount of insulation after the first inch or so becomes much more important in determining the overall U-value of the skin than the rest of the skin assembly. (See ASHRAE for a listing of the thermal resistance of building materials, p. 357, or McGuinness et al., p. 107.)

As a first rule of thumb, consider the insulation levels suggested on the map. (See Bal-

comb, p. 13, for more discussion of balancing energy conservation with the use of solar energy.) In skin-load-dominated, passively cooled buildings, insulation may be more important for reducing solar heat gain than for reducing temperature-caused loads through the skin. Therefore, the roof, with its large solar load, may be very well insulated, while the walls may be only moderately insulated. Buildings in cool climates that have a cooling load because they generate so much internal heat can be "poorly" insulated to increase the rate of heat loss. When using low levels of insulation in cold climates, it is important to keep in mind that the insulation also plays a role in keeping wall surface temperatures warm. Warm walls increase comfort by reducing drafts and reducing the area of cold surfaces within the occupants' radiant field.

Because glazing is more thermally transparent than insulated skin, much more heat flows through the glazing, per unit of area, than through the insulated skin. *The overall U-value for a combination of insulated and single-glazed skin may be found in the graphs called "Heat flow through the skin per square foot of floor area." Enter the left-hand horizontal axis with an area-weighted average U-value of the opaque skin. Move vertically to the diagonal line that represents the percentage of skin area in single glazing. Then move horizontally*

to the vertical axis to find the overall U-value of the glazed and opaque wall. Continue horizontally to the diagonal line that represents the ratio of the exposed skin area to floor area; then drop down to the right-hand horizontal axis to determine the heat flow through the skin in Btu per hr. F° per sq. ft. of building floor area. Since double glazing insulates about twice as well as single glazing, you can use this graph for double glazing by assuming a percentage of glazing equal to one-half of the actual glazing area. Also note that this graph can be used in the reverse order; starting from the overall heat flow you can determine the U-value for the opaque skin.

Heat loss through the skin by building type is listed in Combining Climate, Program, and Form, Technique 18.

	U	R
very well insulated	.02 to .07	14 to 50
well insulated	.07 to .11	9 to 14
insulated	.11 to .17	6 to 9
poorly insulated	.17 +	less than 6

Insulation Levels – Opaque Envelope

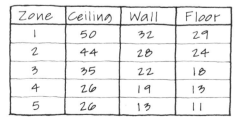

Zone	Ceiling	Wall	Floor
1	50	32	29
2	44	28	24
3	35	22	18
4	26	19	13
5	26	13	11

Recommended Minimum Thermal Resistances (R) of Insulation

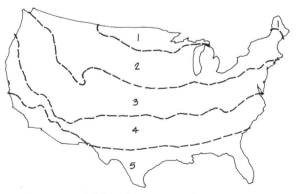

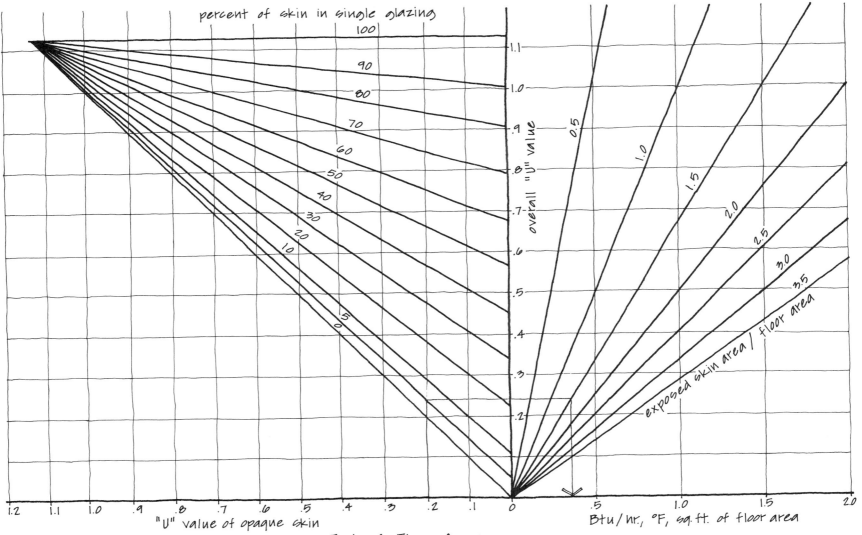

percent of skin in single glazing

100
90
80
70
60
50
40
30
20
10
5
0

overall "U" value

1.1
1.0
.9
.8
.7
.6
.5
.4
.3
.2

0.5
1.0
1.5
2.0
2.5
3.0
3.5

exposed skin area / floor area

"U" value of opaque skin

1.2 1.1 1.0 .9 .8 .7 .6 .5 .4 .3 .2 .1 0 .5 1.0 1.5 2.0

Btu/hr., °F, sq.ft. of floor area

Heat Flow through the Skin per Square Foot of Floor Area

SOLAR GAIN

15. *Estimate the rate of solar heat gain to understand the sun's contribution to the building's heating and cooling requirements.*

The amount of solar radiation transmitted through the skin of a building is a function of the available radiation and the area, orientation, and heat transmission characteristics of the exposed skin. If the skin is opaque, 0 to 12% of the available solar heat will eventually reach the interior spaces, depending on the color of the exterior surface and its insulating qualities.

While solar heat gain through opaque surfaces can be large, especially through poorly insulated roofs, it is usually small compared to the solar gain through glazing, which can be as high as 85% of the incident radiation. The amount of radiation available from clear skies can be found in ASHRAE, p. 388, and Mazria, p. 444, tabulated by latitude, month, time of day, and orientation in Btu per hr. per sq. ft. Clear day radiation data are used to predict the heat gain through the skin for the "worst case" cooling situation. Average conditions can be roughly approximated by adjusting the clear day data by the percentage of possible sunshine for the month listed in *Local Climatological Data, Annual Summary with Comparative Data* (U.S. Dept. of Commerce) for your location. For example, if the clear day radiation for your latitude is 300 Btu per hr. per sq. ft. and the percentage of possible sunshine for your location is 60%, multiply 300 by .60 to find the average radiation of 180 Btu per hr. per sq. ft. Average radiation data for 80 locations can be found in Kusuda and Ishii, *Hourly Solar Radiation Data for Vertical and Horizontal Surfaces on Average Days in the U.S. and Canada.*

The solar radiation striking the glazing should be reduced by the shading coefficient of the glazing itself and of the internal and external shading devices (ASHRAE, p. 400; Olgyay, p. 68).

To determine the solar heat gain through a part of the building skin, select the solar radiation data for the appropriate orientation, slope, hour, latitude, and month. *Find this in the graph on the horizontal axis and draw a line up until it intersects the diagonal line corresponding to the percentage of glazing in the roof or wall. Next, move horizontally until you intersect the diagonal line corresponding to the product of the shading coefficients for the glazing and the shading devices. (If only the glazing or only shades are present, use just the* **one** *shading coefficient corresponding to either the glass or shade.) Drop down to the horizontal axis to read the heat gain through the skin per square foot.* (These values do not include the gain through the opaque section of the skin.)

Multiply the heat gain in Btu per square foot of skin by the area of skin to determine the solar heat gain for that entire surface. Complete this procedure for each surface for the same time and date. Then add these solar heat gains and divide the sum by the number of square feet in the building to determine the solar heat gain per square foot of floor area for that particular month and time of day.

The solar heat gain in Btu per hr. per sq. ft. of floor area for a particular building form and glazing ratio has been calculated for different climates in Combining Climate, Program, and Form, Technique 18.

glass	
clear	.71 – .87
tinted	.45 – .74
heat absorbing	.34 – .83
interior shades	
venetian blinds	.45 – .55
curtains	.40 – .60
exterior shades	
egg crate	.10
horizontal overhang	.2 – .5
vertical fins	.10 – .30
awnings	.15

Shading Coefficients

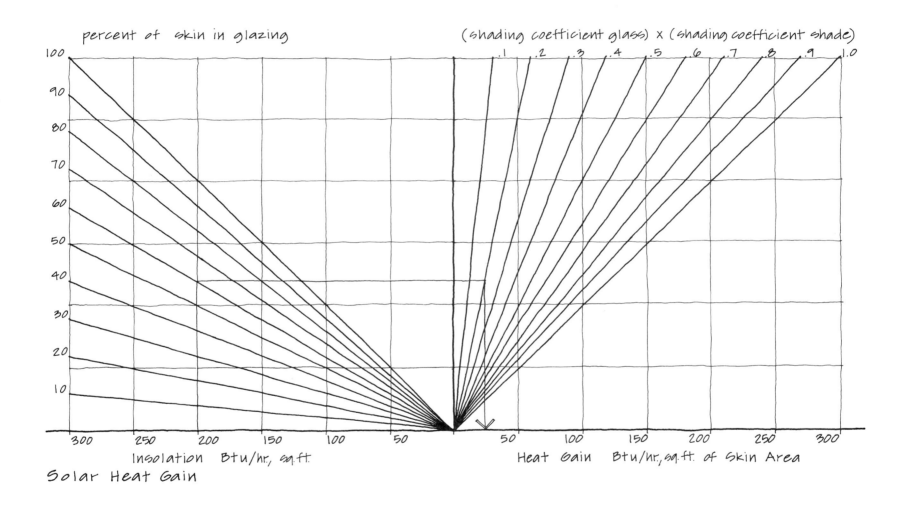

percent of skin in glazing

(shading coefficient glass) x (shading coefficient shade)

.1   .2   .3   .4   .5   .6   .7   .8   .9 1.0

100
90
80
70
60
50
40
30
20
10

300   250   200   150   100   50   50   100   150   200   250   300

Insolation   Btu/hr, sq.ft.

Heat Gain   Btu/hr, sq.ft. of Skin Area

Solar Heat Gain

VENTILATION AND INFILTRATION HEAT GAIN AND LOSS

16. *Estimate the rate of heat gain and loss due to infiltration and ventilation to understand its contribution to the building's heating and cooling requirements.*

Whenever the inside temperature of a building is higher or lower than the outside temperature, air that leaks into the building (infiltration) or is drawn into it for fresh air (ventilation) must be either heated or cooled. In passively heated or cooled buildings that are well-insulated and maintain a substantial difference in temperature between inside and outside and in buildings with a high occupancy level, the heating and cooling of outside air can become a significant part of the thermal load.

The table presents the heat loss and gain in Btu per hr. per F° per sq. ft. of building floor area by building type and residential construction. These values are averages and can easily vary by 50%.

For heat gain that imposes a cooling load on the building, the values are for sensible heat only and do not include the energy that would be necessary for dehumidification. Dehumidification is not possible in most passive cooling systems but would be an important part of cooling loads in conventional refrigeration systems.

clinic hospital retail store	.10
community center hotel / motel warehouse	.02
gymnasium library nursing home office school	.05
restaurant dining area	.20
restaurant kitchen sports arena theater / auditorium	1.0
residential	
insulated frame construction	.3
plus plastic vapor barrier	.2
plus sealed joints, foamed cracks	.1
plus more carefully sealed, and heat recovery unit	.05

based on minimum outside air requirements, ASHRAE, Applications Handbook, 1982, p. 3
Ventilation/Infiltration Gain/Loss
Btu/hr, °F, sq. ft. of floor area

D

Combining Climate, Program, and Form

While each of the analysis techniques outlined in this book may be used separately, many of them are designed to be used together to form the base of data for Technique 19 in Heating and Cooling Patterns. Because climate and occupancy change over the day and the season and because they both interact with the building form, heating and cooling requirements are difficult to predict, making it hard to select appropriate daylighting and passive solar heating and cooling strategies. Analysis Technique 19 helps the designer identify which of three generic heating and cooling patterns applies for different times of the year and under different occupancy conditions. Once the generic patterns have been identified, the appropriate heating, cooling, and daylighting strategies can be determined.

Analysis Technique 18 helps the designer determine the exterior temperature at which the building makes the transition from a heating need to a cooling need for the particular conditions of climate, form, and program. This temperature can then be compared to the outside temperature to see if the building needs heating or cooling. Tables are organized by building type and list rates of heat gain and loss for quick estimates of the transition temperature. These same rates can be used to develop the generic patterns in Technique 19.

If the building is residential or does not generate much internal heat, Technique 17 in Bioclimatic Design Strategies can be used to determine the most appropriate passive solar heating and cooling strategies.

BIOCLIMATIC DESIGN STRATEGIES

17. *Potential passive solar heating and cooling strategies appropriate for your climate can be identified by plotting monthly temperatures and relative humidities on the bioclimatic chart.*

On the bioclimatic chart, plot two points: first, the average minimum temperature for one month by the maximum relative humidity; second, maximum temperature by minimum relative humidity. Connect these points with a straight line and repeat the process for each month of the year. Each line represents the change in temperature and relative humidity over an average day. (See Technique 10 for a more complete explanation of this procedure and the bioclimatic chart.)

The bioclimatic chart is subdivided into zones that define passive solar heating and cooling strategies, based on the work of Milne and Givoni (Watson, p. 96). Note that this older version of the chart differs in form but not in concept from the more recent version by Arens et al. (shown in Technique 10). The zones crossed by the lines you have just plotted indicate the strategies that may be appropriate for your climate. In most U.S. climates, there will be a seasonal change from one strategy to another. Furthermore, some months may lend themselves to several different strategies. In most cases, to reduce costs, the designer should select a few strategies that are compatible with each other and with other design issues.

The design strategies suggested by this version of the bioclimatic chart are only appropriate for residences and other buildings with small internal heat gains. A residential rate of heat gain is assumed to be about 20,000 Btu per day per person. These residential strate-

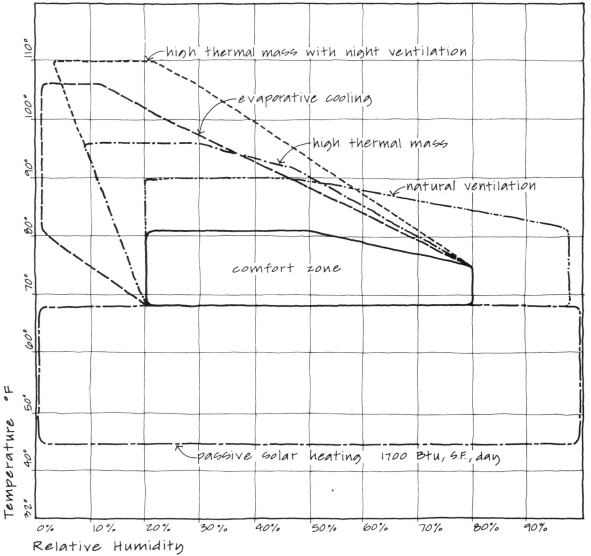

Bioclimatic Chart with Design Strategies

gies are illustrated and described in more detail in Part Two.

Passive solar heating is usually an appropriate strategy for months when the plotted lines fall below the comfort zone. The passive solar heating zone is based on clear day radiation values and certain assumptions about glazing areas and insulation levels. The zone may be extended to lower temperatures depending on building design, radiation levels, and the desired percentage of the annual heating load to be supplied by solar energy.

There are four cooling strategies represented by the four somewhat overlapping zones above the comfort zone. These are: natural ventilation, which depends solely on air movement to cool occupants; large thermal mass, which depends on the building's materials to store heat during the day and reradiate it at night; large thermal mass combined with night ventilation, which relies on mass-heat storage during the day and ventilation at night to cool the mass; and evaporative cooling, which lowers the indoor air temperature by evaporating water in the space.

All of these strategies fall into one of three general categories: open, closed, and open/closed. The open building strategy depends on its connection to the outside wind environment, the closed building depends on its isolation from the exterior temperature environment, and the open/closed building operates in different modes at different times of the day.

As the annual plots for Charleston, South Carolina, Phoenix, Arizona, and Madison, Wisconsin, indicate, the design strategies are quite different for each climate. In Charleston, natural ventilation and solar heating are most appropriate. In Phoenix, high mass with night ventilation and evaporative cooling are good strategies for cooling, and heating can be done effectively by the sun. In Madison, natural ventilation will meet cooling needs and the sun will meet some of the heating needs.

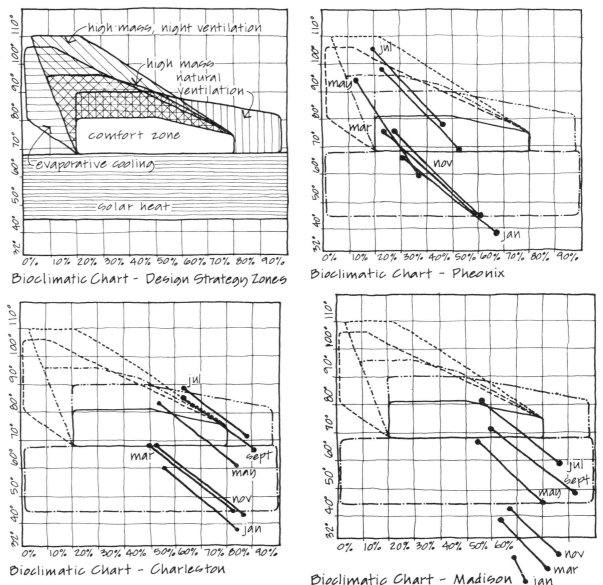

Bioclimatic Chart - Design Strategy Zones

Bioclimatic Chart - Pheonix

Bioclimatic Chart - Charleston

Bioclimatic Chart - Madison

HEATING AND COOLING PATTERNS

18. *The outside temperature at which the building makes a transition from a heating need to a cooling need can be calculated and used to determine when heating and cooling are required.*

The "balance point" for a building is defined as the outdoor temperature at which the heat generated inside the building balances the building's heat loss, to maintain a desired inside temperature. If the balance point of a building is 50°F, then the building must be cooled when the outside temperature is above 50°F and heated when the temperature is below 50°F. The balance point is a function of the rate of heat gain in the building from people, equipment, lights, and solar radiation and the rate of heat loss by ventilation and conduction. (See ASHRAE, Ch. 3.) Since the amount of heat loss is a function of the difference in temperature between the inside and outside, the building will lose as much heat as it produces at a sufficiently low temperature, the balance point. The rate of heat gain inside the building changes over the day or week or year due to occupancy patterns and available solar radiation. The rate of heat loss may also change due to varying ventilation rates related to occupancy or changes in the insulating quality of the skin from day to night. Because only passive systems are being considered here, only *sensible* heat is included in calculations.

Once the balance point has been determined, it can be compared to the outside temperature for any time period to see how the building's need for heating and cooling changes. This information can be used to determine when to use design strategies for passive solar heating, cooling, and daylighting.

To determine the balance point of a building, enter the graph on the vertical axis with the rate of heat gain in Btu per hr. per sq. ft. of building floor area. Next, draw a horizontal line until it intersects the diagonal line corresponding to the building's rate of heat loss in Btu per hr. per F° per sq. ft. of building floor area. From that point drop vertically to the horizontal axis. Read here the temperature differences (ΔT) between inside and outside at which a particular rate of heat gain given will balance heat loss. To determine the exterior balance point temperature, subtract the ΔT found on the horizontal axis from the desired interior temperature.

Inside temp. $- \Delta T =$ Balance point temp.

The rates of heat gain and loss can be approximated by using Techniques 11, 12, 13, 14, 15, and 16, or by summing the rates of heat gain from lights, people, equipment, and the sun and heat loss from ventilation/infiltration and through the skin as listed in the tables for various building types.

The rates of heat loss and gain by building type were developed by Don Harton on the basis of many assumptions about building form, envelope construction, occupancy, lighting levels, etc., so they should only be used as a rough guide. They may, in fact, be quite misleading if just one or two key assumptions in your building design are different. On the other hand, they are a place to start if you have limited time or you are working with an unfamiliar climate or building type.

The solar gain for your building is likely to be quite different from the charts if your glazing isn't 12% of the floor area, equally distributed in a building with square plan. If the amount of glazing is smaller, it is well shaded, and the building is large, variations from these assumptions may not be too important. If the glazing area is larger and the building is small, then deviations from the assumptions probably will be substantial. In most cases the assumptions are conservative; that is, they will tend to overstate the rate of both heat gain and heat loss.

The cities listed in the chart were selected on the basis of both heating-degree days and typical available solar radiation. Select the city that most closely matches your own.

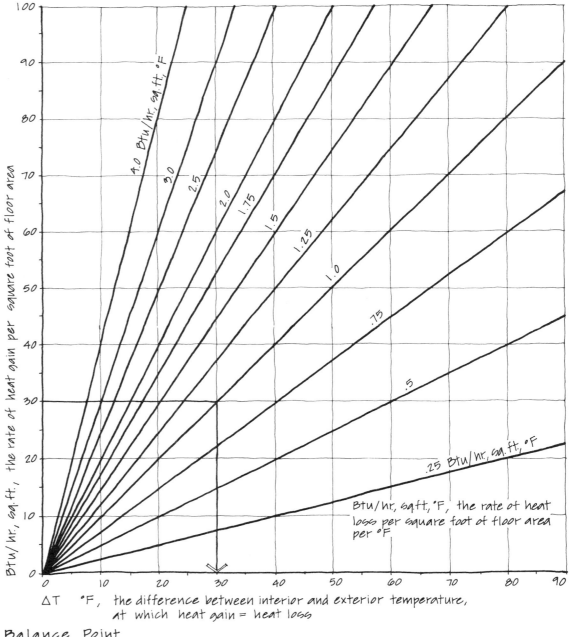

Btu/hr, sq. ft., the rate of heat gain per square foot of floor area

ΔT   °F, the difference between interior and exterior temperature,
         at which heat gain = heat loss

Btu/hr, sq.ft., °F, the rate of heat
loss per square foot of floor area
per °F

Balance Point

Building Type	Btu/hr, sqft
clinic	23
community center	8
gymnasium	5
hospital	34
hotel/motel	8
library	20
nursing home	16
office (computerized)	38
office	19
residence (single family)	7
residence (multi family)	7
restaurant (dining area)	29
restaurant (kitchen)	59
school (elementary)	16
school (secondary/university)	14
shopping center	19
shopping (detached)	20
sports arena	39
theater / auditorium	32
warehouse	2

Heat Gain from Lights, People and Equipment, Btu/hr, sq. ft of Floor Area

Season	Hour	Charleston, SC	Dodge City, KS	Madison, WI	Phoenix AZ
winter	06	0	0	0	0
	09	6	7	4	8
	12	5	6	4	7
	15	6	7	4	8
	18	0	0	0	0
spring	06	2	3	3	2
	09	6	6	5	8
	12	4	4	4	5
	15	6	6	5	8
	18	2	3	3	2
summer	06	3	4	4	4
	09	5	6	6	7
	12	3	4	4	4
	15	5	6	6	7
	18	3	4	4	4
fall	06	0	0	0	0
	09	7	7	6	9
	12	6	7	5	7
	15	7	7	6	9
	18	0	0	0	0

assumes: double glazing equal to 12% of floor area equally distributed on four sides of a square building which is unshaded; solar gain through opaque surfaces is neglected; clear sky radiation has been reduced by the percentage of possible sunshine; maximum area per floor is 100,000 sq. ft.

Solar Heat Gain, Btu/hr, sq. ft. of floor area

Building Type	Floor Area, Sq.Ft No. of Floors	Charleston, SC and Phoenix, AZ	Dodge City, KS	Madison WI
clinic, community center, hospital, hotel, motel, library, nursing home, office (computerized), office, restaurant dining, restaurant kitchen, secondary school, elementary school, university and warehouse	1,000 / 1	.7	.6	.5
	2,000 / 1	.5	.4	.4
	5,000 / 1	.4	.3	.2
	10,000 / 1	.3	.2	.2
	60,000 / 1	.2	.1	.1
	60,000 / 3	.2	.1	.1
	100,000 / 5	.2	.1	.1
	200,000 / 5	.1	.1	.1
	200,000 / 10	.1	.1	.1
	500,000 / 25	.2	.1	.1
multi- and single- family residential	1,000 / 1	.5	.4	.3
	2,000 / 1	.3	.3	.2
	5,000 / 1	.3	.2	.1
	60,000 / 3	.1	.1	.1
	100,000 / 5	.1	.1	.1
	200,000 / 10	.1	.1	.1
	500,000 / 25	.1	.1	.1
gymnasium, shopping mall and detached shopping	1,000 / 1	1.4	1.2	1.0
	2,000 / 1	1.0	.9	.7
	5,000 / 1	.6	.6	.5
	10,000 / 1	.5	.4	.4
	60,000 / 1	.3	.2	.2
	60,000 / 3	.3	.3	.2
sports arena, theater and auditorium	5,000 / 1	1.2	1.1	.9
	10,000 / 1	.9	.8	.7
	60,000 / 1	.4	.4	.3

assumes: overall 'u'-values are similar to ASHRAE 90-75

Heat Loss Through the Skin, Btu/hr, °F, Sq. Ft. of Floor Area

Building Type	Btu/hr, °F, sq.ft.
clinic, hospital, shopping mall and detached shopping	.1
community center, hotel, motel, single- and multi-family residential and warehouse	.02
gymnasium, library, nursing home, office and school	.05
restaurant dining	.2
restaurant kitchen, sports arena, theater and auditorium	1.0

based on minimum outside air requirements, ASHRAE, Applications Handbook, 1982, p.3

Heat Loss by Ventilation/Infiltration, Btu/hr, °F, sq. ft. of floor area

HEATING AND COOLING PATTERNS

19. *The characteristics of the climate, the building's use, and the building's form can be used to develop a series of daily heating and cooling patterns that represent the building's performance over a year and help identify daylighting and passive heating and cooling design strategies.*

The purpose of identifying the generic heating and cooling patterns that apply to your building is to establish appropriate design strategies while the design is still in its most formative stages. Graphs may be generated using precise data or rough approximations. They will only be as accurate as the data used to generate them, but they take much more time to do precisely than roughly. Since at the beginning of the design process we are interested in identifying the basic types of patterns and their related design strategies, the extra effort required for precision may not be worth the time it takes. By doing the graph roughly the first time and with increasing precision and detail for successive trials, you can get an idea of the relationship between effort in and usable information out.

The process for generating the generic heating and cooling patterns has ten steps. 1. Select months of the year to analyze. 2. Plot the outside temperature for an average day in those months. 3. Assume a hypothetical building form. 4. For that building, determine the heat gain from people, lights, equipment, and the sun. 5. Determine heat loss through the envelope and infiltration/ventilation. 6. Determine when the building is occupied so that you can tell when lights, equipment, etc. will be turned on. 7. Determine the heat gain and loss at four-hour intervals during the day. 8. Use the heat gain and loss to determine the balance point temperature for each four-hour

interval. 9. Plot the balance point temperatures on the same graphs as the average outside temperature, and develop the generic heating and cooling patterns. 10. Use the patterns to identify appropriate types of design strategies.

STEP 1

The first step in the process is to select the months that are representative of your climate. Do the bioclimatic plots shown in Technique 10 if you have doubts about which months may be important. Four months will be analyzed as representative of the Salem, Oregon, climate: January, March, June, and September.

STEP 2

For each month, plot the average high temperature at 4 PM and average low temperature at 4 AM. In Salem, January has an average high of 45 °F and an average low of 32 °F. Connect the high and low with a straight line. The intersection of this line with each vertical time line approximates the temperature at those times. The temerature profile is assumed to be symmetrical around 4 PM, so use the noon temperature to plot the 8 PM temperature, and the 8 AM temperature to plot the midnight temperature (twice).

STEP 3

The next stage in the process is to make some assumptions about the building form. First, develop a simple rectangular shape that represents the building. Consider as much about the site and program as possible with-

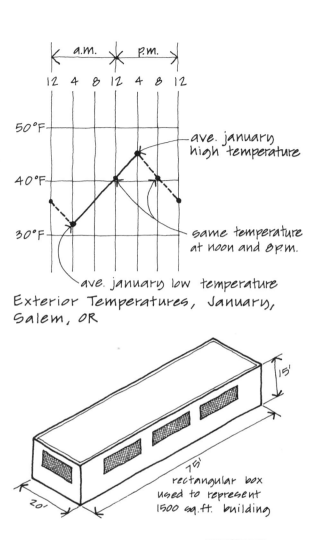

Exterior Temperatures, January, Salem, OR

rectangular box used to represent 1500 sq.ft. building

east and west elevations —glazing 20% of area or 60 sq. ft.

north and south elevations —glazing 20% of area or 225 sq. ft.

Hypothetical Building, 1500 sq. ft.

out going beyond the most basic diagrammatic relationships. Remember the purpose of this analysis is to inform the design, *not* to evaluate after it is finished. For example, the building under construction for the Salem site is a 1,500 sq. ft. office building. A rectangle 20′ × 75′ × 15′ high was used to represent a single-loaded corridor scheme. The building will need good lighting; therefore it's assumed that 20% of the wall area will be single glazing.

STEP 4

The next step is to determine the heat gain from people, light, equipment, and sun. This will include sensible gains only, for passive systems. In office spaces the maximum occupancy is one person per 100 sq. ft. and the average occupancy is one-half to one-third person per 100 sq. ft. Assuming an average occupancy of one-half person per 100 sq. ft. and a sensible heat gain of a moderately active office of 250 Btu per hr., the graph from Technique 11 indicates that heat gain from people will be approximately 1.4 Btu per hr. per sq. ft.

The visual tasks in the office are assumed to be of fairly high contrast, so an overall illumination level of 50 footcandles is selected from the chart from Technique 12. Fluorescent lighting will be the predominant light source. The graph from Technique 12 indicates that 50 footcandles of light from fluorescent lights produces approximately 11.9 Btu per hr. per sq. ft. From the chart from Technique 13, we estimate the heat gain from office equipment to be 3 Btu per hr. per sq. ft. Using data from Kusuda and Ishii, *Hourly Solar Radiation Data for Vertical and Horizontal Surfaces on Average Days in the United States and Canada,* for the nearest city, Medford, Oregon, the radia-

tion levels in Btu per hr. per sq. ft. for January are shown in the table.

	8 AM	Noon	4 PM
South facing	27	105	27
West facing	6	27	36
North facing	6	27	6
East facing	36	27	6
Horizontal	14	79	14

If your city is not listed in Kusuda and Ishii, then you can approximate this information using Technique 15.

The hypothetical building design has 20% glazing on all elevations and no glazing in the roof. The shading coefficient of the glass is assumed to be .80 and there are no interior or exterior shades. Using the graph from Technique 15, enter the horizontal axis with the radiation from one hour and one orientation in the above table. Move vertically to the diagonal line that represents 20% glazing; reflect horizontally to the diagonal .8 shading coefficient line; then reflect down to the horizontal axis and read the heat gain per sq. ft. of skin for that time and wall orientation. Using that process, the following heat gain in Btu per sq. ft. was determined for each elevation for each hour.

	8 AM	Noon	4 PM
South elevation	4	17	4
West elevation	1	4	6
North elevation	1	4	1
East elevation	6	4	1
Roof (no glazing)	0	0	0

The next step is to multiply the heat gain per sq. ft. of skin times the amount of skin in each elevation. In the hypothetical example,

the area of the north and south elevations is 1,125 sq. ft., and the east and west elevations are 300 sq. ft. The heat gain in Btu per skin area is as follows:

	8 AM	Noon	4 PM
South elevation	4,500	19,125	4,500
West elevation	300	1,200	1,800
North elevation	1,125	4,500	1,125
East elevation	1,800	1,200	300
Roof	0	0	0
TOTAL	7,725	26,025	7,725

Next, divide the total heat gain for all skin areas for each hour by the floor area (1,500 sq. ft.) to determine the heat gain per area of building.

Heat gain in Btu per hr. per sq. ft. of floor area

8 AM	Noon	4 PM
5.2	17.4	5.2

STEP 5

The next step in the process is to determine the rate of heat loss from the building due to infiltration/ventilation and transfer through the skin. Since this office is small and will probably be constructed with residential methods, .18 Btu per hr. per F° per sq. ft. was used (see Technique 16) as the rate of heat loss (or gain, if the outside air were hotter than inside).

The office is assumed to be well-insulated, with an average opaque skin U-value of .09 Btu per hr. per F° per sq. ft. (See Technique 14.) The floor slab has been neglected because its losses are assumed to be small. To adjust this value to include the glazing, which

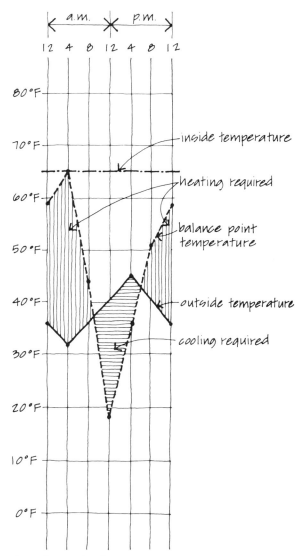

a.m. p.m.
12 4 8 12 4 8 12

80°F
70°F — inside temperature
60°F — heating required
50°F — balance point temperature
40°F — outside temperature
30°F — cooling required
20°F
10°F
0°F

Combined Exterior and Balance
Point Temperatures, January,
Salem, OR

is 20% of the exposed skin area, use the graph from Technique 14 to determine the overall U-value of .19 Btu per hr. per F° per sq. ft. Next determine the ratio of the exposed skin area to the floor area. The wall area is (2 × 20′ × 15′) + (2 × 75′ × 15′) or 2,850 sq. ft. The roof is 1,500 sq. ft., making a total exposed skin area of 4,350 sq. ft. The skin area divided by the floor area is 4,350/ 1,500 = 2.9. Use the graph from Technique 14 to determine the heat loss of .55 Btu per hr. per F° per sq. ft. of building floor area.

The total rate of heat loss from the office is the ventilation/infiltration rate plus the loss through the skin: .18 + .55 = .73 Btu per hr. per F° per sq. ft.

STEP 6

Once the rates of heat gain and loss have been determined, an average occupancy schedule should be completed for the hours of the day for each month of the year under consideration. (Any hours of the day can be used, and unusual conditions as well as average ones can be graphed.) The four-hour intervals on the daily graphs are used in this example.

STEP 7

Sum the heat gains for each time period. Next, determine the average inside temperature. Plot the average inside temperature on the daily graph. For our example, we assume an interior temperature of 65°F all day.

STEP 8

Use the rate of heat gain for each hour, the total rate of heat loss, and the balance point chart from Technique 18 to determine the ΔT and balance point temperature for each hour. For example, at 8 PM the rate of gain is 9.7 Btu per hr. per sq. ft., and rate of loss is .73 Btu per hr. per sq. ft. The balance point chart reveals that the ΔT is 14°. Subtracting 14° from the inside temperature of 65°, the balance point is determined to be 51°F. The following balance points were determined in a similar manner.

JANUARY

	People	Lights	Equip.	Solar	Total
12 mid.	0	3†	0	0	3
4 AM	0	0	0	0	0
8 AM	.7*	6**	3	5.2	14.9
12 noon	1.4	11.9	3	17.4	33.7
4 PM	1.4	11.9	3	5.2	21.5
8 PM	.7*	6**	3	0	9.7
12 mid.	0	3†	0	0	3

Heat gains in Btu per hr.
per sq. ft. of floor area

 * One-half the people have arrived or left.
 † 25% of the lights are on for cleaning.
** 50% of the lights are on as people arrive and leave.

Hour	Gain	Loss	ΔT	Inside − ΔT	= Bal. pt F°
12 mid.	3	.73	6	65 − 6	59
4 AM	0	.73	0	65 − 0	65
8 AM	14.9	.73	21	65 − 21	44
12 noon	33.7	.73	47	65 − 47	18
4 PM	21.5	.73	30	65 − 30	35
8 PM	9.7	.73	14	65 − 14	51
12 mid.	3	.73	6	65 − 6	59

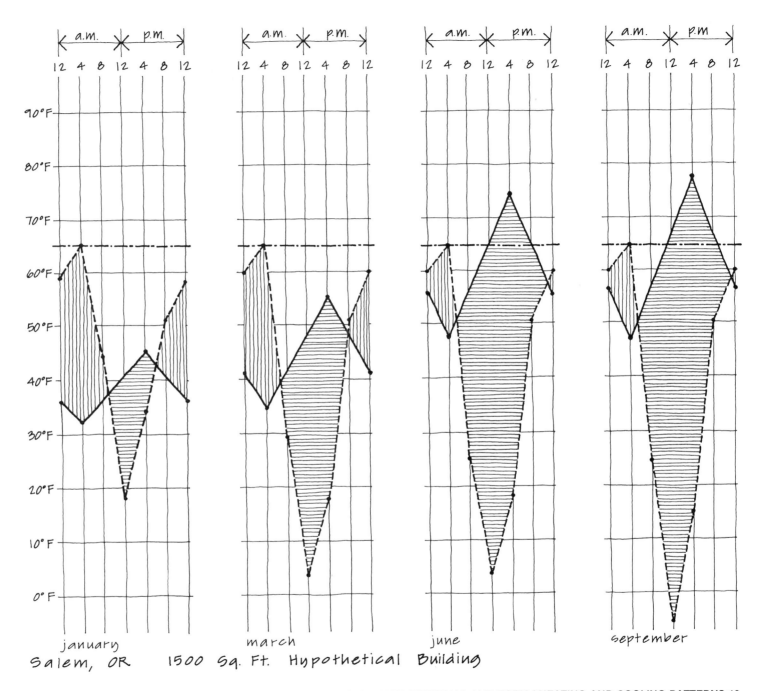

january   march   june   september

Salem, OR   1500 Sq. Ft. Hypothetical Building

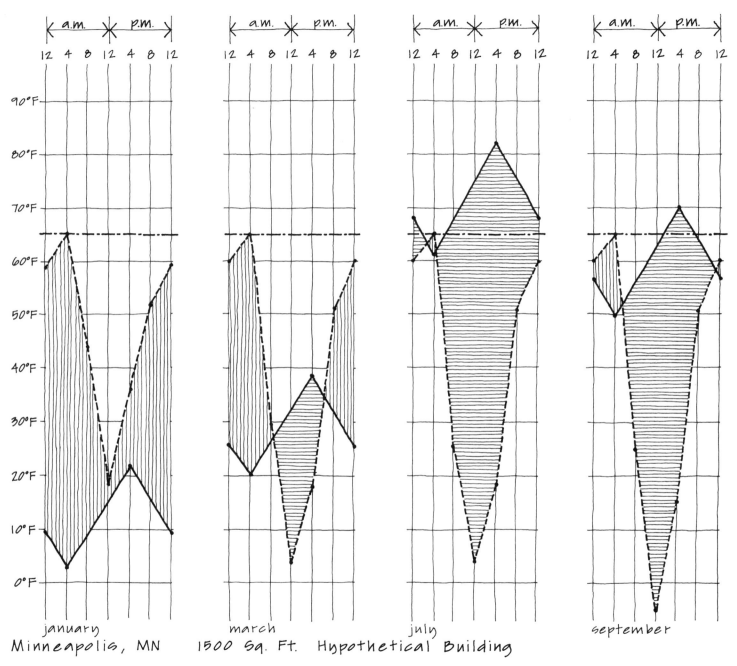

january   march   july   september

Minneapolis, MN   1500 Sq. Ft. Hypothetical Building

Energy conservation strategies table — column groups (numbered columns):

- interior temperature: 1. increase, 2. decrease
- internal heat generation: 3. increase, 4. decrease
- solar heat gain: 5. increase, 6. decrease
- rate of heat flow through the envelope gain or loss: 7. increase, 8. decrease
- rate of heat transfer by ventilation gain or loss: 9. increase, 10. decrease
- storage: 11. store heat, 12. store cold

Condition		1. increase	2. decrease	3. increase	4. decrease	5. increase	6. decrease	7. increase	8. decrease	9. increase	10. decrease	11. store heat	12. store cold
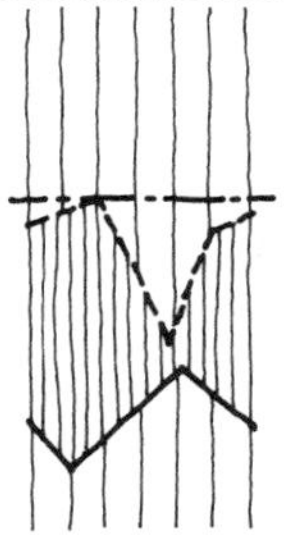 heating always required			X	X		X			X	X			
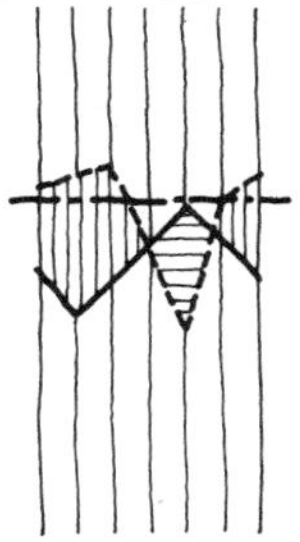 heating and cooling required	heating		X	X		X			X		X		X
	cooling— outside temperature above inside	X			X		X		X		X	X	
	cooling— outside temperature below inside	X			X		X	X		X		X	
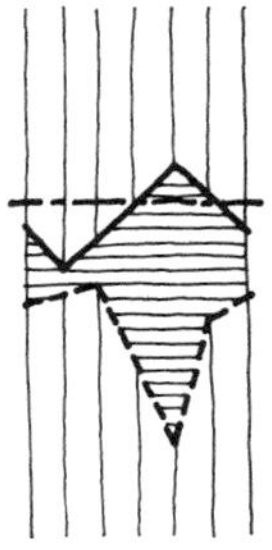 cooling always required	outside temperature above inside	X			X		X		X		X		
	outside temperature below inside	X			X		X	X		X			X

Energy Conservation Strategies

STEP 9

Plot the balance points on the same graph on which you plotted the outside temperatures.

STEP 10

When the balance point temperature exceeds the outside temperature, the building needs to be heated; when the outside temperature exceeds the balance point temperature, the building needs to be cooled. For the hypothetical building in Salem in January, the heat gain from people, lights, equipment, and the sun exceeds the heat loss during much of the day, and the heat loss exceeds the heat gain during most of the night.

Following the same procedures, graphs have been prepared for the three remaining months.

The graphs for March, June, and September illustrate a similar pattern: cooling requirements during the day and heating requirements at night, though in September, the heating requirements are greatly diminished and the cooling requirements are accentuated. The building load is clearly internally dominated—what happens inside the building in terms of heat gain is more important than what happens outside in terms of climate.

A similar building located in Minneapolis, Minnesota, performs quite differently and is more greatly influenced by the climate. In January the building needs to be heated all the time. In March and September it needs to be heated some of the time and cooled some of the time, and in July it needs to be cooled almost all the time.

These are the three basic generic patterns: heating need alone, cooling need alone, and both heating and cooling need together in one day. For each pattern there is an associated set of strategies for energy conservation. First, identify the patterns that are appropriate for your building and then look across the row to see which strategies are appropriate. There are six groups of strategies, each of which is divided into two parts. The first strategy, adjust the interior temperature, is based on the simple idea that the smaller the temperature difference between inside and out, the less energy will be required to heat or cool the building. This can be accomplished by allowing the temperature to fluctuate during unoccupied periods, say between 50 and 90°F; grouping activities together that have a high tolerance for temperature fluctuations, say between 60 and 80°F; and allowing the interior temperature to vary with the season, say 65° in the winter and 78° in the summer.

In the second strategy, internal heat generation, internal sources of heat can be increased to help offset the heating load and decreased to decrease the cooling load. Daylighting is an excellent example of reducing the internal heat generated by decreasing the heat generated by electric lights.

The third strategy, solar heat gain, indicates that solar heat can be used to offset the heating load by, for example, increasing the area of south-facing glazing. It can also be decreased by shading devices to reduce the cooling requirements.

The fourth, rate of heat flow through the envelope—gain or loss, indicates that the rate of heat flow can be increased by reducing the amount of insulation. This is an advantage if the building has a cooling requirement and the outside temperature is lower than the inside temperature. It is a disadvantage if the outside temperature is higher than the inside temperature. When the outside temperature is less than the inside temperature and heating is required, it is an advantage to decrease the heat flow through the envelope. The fifth strategy, rate of heat transfer by ventilation—gain or loss, is similar to manipulating the rate of flow through the envelope.

The sixth strategy, storage, is useful when a building has both a heating and cooling requirement in the same day. When excess heat is available during the cooling phase, it can be stored in the mass of the structure or remotely and used to heat the structure later in the day. When the outside temperature is sometimes below the inside temperature in buildings that always have a cooling load, the cold may be stored in the building's structure or remotely to help offset the cooling load when the outside temperature rises above the inside temperature. A more detailed listing of energy conversation strategies in each of the six categories is in the Department of Energy's publication *Predesign Energy Analysis.*

It is important to realize that all the strategies suggested for a particular pattern are not necessarily compatible with each other and that over the course of the year different months or days will exhibit different patterns that have mutually exclusive design strategies. The designer's goal should be to identify the strategies that address the problems that occur the most often and have the potential for addressing multiple problems.

PART TWO
DESIGN STRATEGIES

The goal of this section is to identify a comprehensive yet limited set of design strategies to use in the schematic part of the design process. They must be comprehensive so that no major opportunities are missed, but they also have to be few enough in number that they are memorable and do not bury the designer in too much information. I used five criteria to evaluate whether or not a design strategy should be included in this book. First, of course, it must deal with energy; second, it must be primarily passive in nature. The term "passive" is defined rather loosely, and many of the illustrations are hybrid schemes, using some energy for pumps, fans, and controls. Third, the strategies must reveal major form and organizational relationships. This criterion eliminates a large number of very good energy-conservation strategies. For example, it eliminates the strategy of using plastic vapor barriers to reduce infiltration. This is an extremely important consideration in the design of any solar-heated building because infiltration is a major source of heat loss. However, because vapor barriers are thin and usually concealed in the wall, their consideration can easily be left to later stages of the design process. In many cases, if things don't take much space or have very specific locations they don't require exacting consideration in the scheming stage because the consequences of changing them later in the design process are not very great.

As a fourth criterion, even if a strategy doesn't reveal a major form or organizational relationship, it is included if it has a potentially major impact on the appearance of the building. Two examples are the way certain daylighting strategies limit the possible solid/void relationships on the facades and the way masonry tends to be used for thermal storage on the interior surfaces rather than on exterior surfaces. Fifth, some small-scale strategies are included if ignoring them at the schematic stages would require redesign in later design stages. An example of this is night insulation—certainly an important energy-conserving strategy but probably not one that reveals major relationships. However, because storing the insulation can prove to be such a sticky problem later on in the design process, it is worth taking into account at the beginning.

The design strategies are organized first by three scales; building groups, buildings, and building parts. Most of the principles underlying energy phenomena do not change much within this scale range but their manifestations can. For example, while the sun's movement remains the same at all scales, the designer's thoughts about the sun's movement might be quite different at each scale. At the building groups scale, the concern might be how to arrange buildings and streets to provide solar access; at the building scale, how to arrange major living areas to receive the sun; and at the building parts scale, how to arrange the windows so that the sun penetrates deep into the room. All have to do with sun position and movement but the elements and issues under consideration are quite different at each scale. Some principles are developed in strategies at all scales, but in most cases the principles affect the strategies at just those one or two scales where the principles reveal major form and organizational relationships. With some imagination, the designer can easily extend a strategy from one scale to any other.

One might well expect a book about energy to be organized by categories like daylighting, heating, and cooling, and by subjects like ventilation and shading. These organizations are important and the indexes provide access to the contents by energy subject. However, in the schematic design stage, designers aren't thinking in an orderly fashion about a list of single isolated subjects, but are thinking about multiple subjects simultaneously; furthermore, the designer is thinking about the subjects as secondary while primarily studying the arrangement of architectural elements such as streets, plazas, rooms, and windows. Therefore, in addition to scales, the other major organizing devices for this book are the architectural elements the designer works with.

At the building groups scale they are streets, open spaces, and buildings; at the building scale, rooms and courtyards; at the building parts scale, they are walls, roofs, and windows. The architectural elements are grouped by form characteristics, such as shape, orientation, location, edge, enclosure, size, material, and color, and organizational characteristics, like thin, compact, elongated, dispersed, zoned, and layered.

One way to use this book, when you are considering a particular problem—perhaps how to arrange a group of rooms—is to pursue the strategies at the building scale having to do with organizing rooms as a source of ideas to be included in your design. Another way to use the book, when working with a particular design idea like a compact organization of rooms, is to look up the characteristics of compact arrangements in terms of their potential for heating, cooling, and lighting.

Each design strategy is limited, in most cases, to one or two pages containing a strategy statement, an explanation of the phenomenon related to the strategy, a sizing rule of thumb, and an illustration of the strategy in an architectural application. Each strategy was developed in light of three questions whose answers are necessary to design any physical object: **What** are the architectural elements involved? **What is the relationship** between those elements? and **How big** are the elements? The question of how big was consistently the most difficult to answer appropriately at the schematic design stage. With a couple of exceptions, all strategies where the "how big" question is important have a sizing rule of thumb. Some useful energy-conservation strategies have been discarded because there was no rule of thumb for their sizing.

The strategy statements aren't directive; they don't say that one *must* do this to conserve energy. They do say that if one does this, this will probably be the result. They are stated this way first because the strategies are frequently redundant—the problem can be solved at several scales or with different elements. The strategy that fits with the designer's other concerns should be selected. Second, there is no single right way to do something without the agreement of the people involved and affected; therefore, the strategies are stated as possibilities, not as absolutes.

A

Building Groups

The strategies in the Building Groups section deal with the range of scales that extends beyond the single building to a cluster, block, town, or city. The major architectural elements they address are buildings, streets, and open spaces, which are the primary pieces that make up building groups. The strategies are mostly concerned with relationships between those pieces, either between buildings or between buildings and open spaces/streets.

Several of the strategies (Strategies 20, 21, 26, and 27) are concerned with insuring access of individual areas to the basic ingredients for daylighting and passive solar heating and cooling, that is, the sun, wind, and light. Strategy 22 helps the designer locate building groups in terms of topography and climate.

The remaining strategies involve forming building groups to manipulate the sun (Strategies 23, 28) and the wind (Strategies 23, 24, 25) to improve the microclimates near the buildings.

STREETS, OPEN SPACES, AND BUILDINGS: Shape and Orientation

20. *Solar envelopes can be used to insure access to the sun for buildings, streets and open spaces. [heating and cooling]*

The solar envelope defines the maximum buildable volume for a given site that can be filled without shading adjacent sites, thereby assuring the availability of solar energy to those sites. The size and shape of the solar envelope varies with site size, orientation, and latitude, the times of day solar access is desired, and the amount of allowable shading on adjacent streets and buildings (Knowles, 1981, p. 51).

Once the shape and orientation of the site have been determined, the geometry of the solar envelope is determined by the time period during which solar access must be maintained. For example, to construct a solar envelope for a site at 40° north latitude that provides solar access to adjacent sites between 9 AM and 3 PM all year, select the month when the sun is lowest in the sky (December) to determine the slope of the north part of the envelope and the month when the sun is highest in the sky (June) to determine the slope of the south part of the envelope. Assuming that before 9 AM and after 3 PM shading adjacent sites is permitted, the sun positions at 9 AM and 3 PM on December 21 and June 21 define the maximum size of the solar envelope. At 40° north latitude the sun positions at those times are:

Dec. 21   9 AM and 3 PM:
    Altitude 14°, Azimuth ±42°
June 21   9 AM and 3 PM:
    Altitude 49°, Azimuth ±80°

The diagonal line to the northwest corner is defined by the sun's angle at 9 AM; the diag-

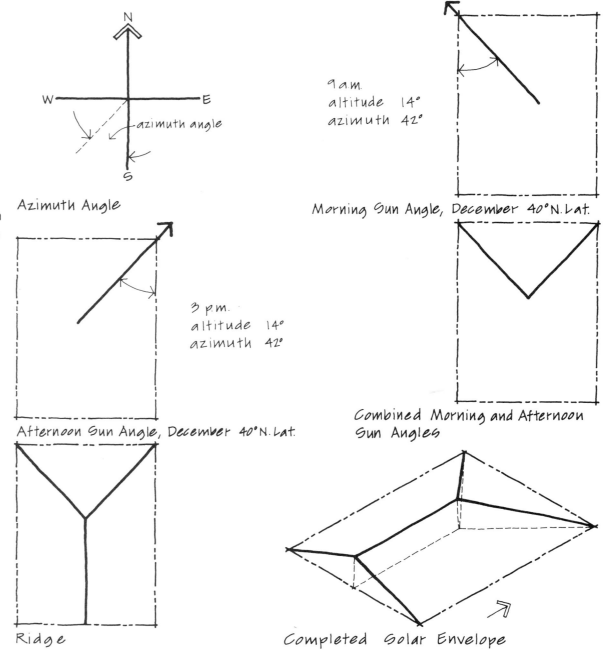

Azimuth Angle

Afternoon Sun Angle, December 40°N. Lat.

Ridge

9 a.m.
altitude 14°
azimuth 42°

3 p.m.
altitude 14°
azimuth 42°

Morning Sun Angle, December 40°N. Lat.

Combined Morning and Afternoon Sun Angles

Completed Solar Envelope

onal to the northeast corner, by the angle at 3 PM. The intersection of the morning and afternoon diagonals forms one end of a potential ridge line. But because the sun at 40° north latitude between 9 AM and 3 PM doesn't get to the north of east or west, it never casts a shadow to south. Therefore, it is assumed that the south face of the solar envelope rises vertically from the edge of the site. If the sun is ever north of east and west at the cutoff times, then the southwest and southeast diagonals are defined by the sun's angle at 9 AM and 3 PM. The ridge line is formed by either the intersection of the winter diagonals or the summer diagonals, whichever is lower in height. The completed envelope defines the maximum building height at any point on the site that will not shade an adjacent site from 9 AM to 3 PM from December 21 to June 21.

To construct the solar envelope for a given rectangular block of cardinal 0° or 45° street orientations, providing solar access from 9 AM to 3 PM:

1) Determine the latitude.
2) Determine or assume the dimensions of the site; the street width or any open space may be included.
3) Find the plan angles of the solar envelope from the table for the correct latitude; draw these angles on a plan of the block.
4) Connect the points of intersection of the plan angles; this represents the ridge.
5a) Cardinal orientation: if the ridge runs north-south find its height in the table as a function of the 'x' or east-west dimension of the site; if there is no ridge or if the ridge runs east-west, find its height in the table as a function of the 'y', the north-south dimension of the site.
5b) 45° orientation: find the ridge height in the table as a function of the shortest dimension.

Ridge Heights of Solar Envelopes — Cardinal Orientation

Variables that affect the configuration of the envelope are the latitude, the period of access, the size of the site, its proportions, slope, orientation, and the nature of its edge conditions. Northern latitudes allow less height and therefore less volume than southern latitudes. Reducing the period of solar access will result in a higher but sharper peak. Increasing the size of the site will decrease the skin-to-volume ratio of the envelope. If the proportions of the site result in a north–south ridge, the envelope will contain less volume to be developed than if the proportions of the site result in an east–west ridge.

On a slope, if the ridge of the envelope runs with the direction of the slope, the ridge height will remain the same. If the ridge runs across the direction of the slope, the ridge height will vary; a south slope will increase the height and all other slopes will decrease the height.

Changing the orientation of a level site, that is, rotating its alignment to 30°, 45°, or 60° off the cardinal orientations, reduces the envelope height and volume.

Finally, the edge condition of the block may be varied to increase the volume of the envelope. The point of solar access may be taken to begin a distance horizontally from the edge of the block (across the street). It may also be taken a distance vertically from street level (the top of a fence). In either case, the effect is to lift the envelope onto a platform. This is particularly viable in dense, multi-use, vertical zoning where higher residential floors may require solar access while lower commercial floors do not. Existing sites often have complex edge conditions that allow a variety of manipulations of the envelope.

Ralph Knowles and his students at the University of Southern California have done extensive design exercises using the solar envelope at various scales (Knowles, 1981, pp. 179-282). *The examples show a small building developed for a corner site using a complex solar envelope that extended beyond the site boundaries.*

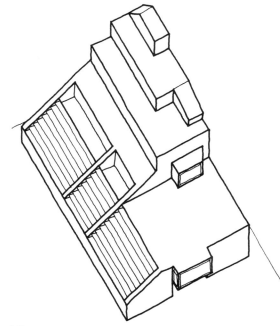

View From Northwest

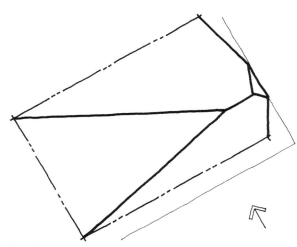

Solar Envelope

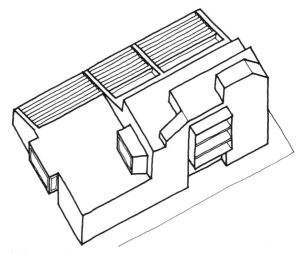

View From Southwest

north ⇑	plan view	x y	x y
48° N. Latitude	45°, 3°, 45°	.12 x	.12 y
40° N. Latitude	45°, 7°, 45°	.22 x	.22 y
32° N. Latitude	45°, 12°, 45	.29 x	.29 y
24° N. Latitude	45°, 18°, 45°	.35 x	.35 y

Ridge Heights of Solar Envelopes — 45° Orientation

21. *Daylight spacing angles can be used to shape and space buildings to assure adequate daylight access to the street and adjacent buildings. [daylighting]*

Daylighting in hot climates that have clear skies and a bright sun involves finding ways to use the light while excluding as much solar heat as possible from the building or open space. *Window area should be limited to 10 to 20% of the wall area (Koenigsberger, p. 244).* Since the exterior illumination is often 500 times more than that required inside, windows are often located so that their *view of the sky dome is obstructed and light is filtered and reflected before it reaches the windows,* as it is in this window overlooking a court shaded by trees in a house in **Dubai, United Arab Emirates** (Coles & Jackson, p. 10).

The light from reflecting surfaces such as the ground or adjacent facades, which are usually light in color to reflect heat away from the building, can easily exceed the illumination from the clear sky without the sun (Hopkinson et al., p. 505). Because the interior light levels are low, even reflected light is a potential source of glare that often should be filtered at the window plane. Indigenous builders in hot arid climates use wood screens called **"mash rabiyya"** to filter the light.

Under overcast sky conditions, the bright sun isn't available and exterior light levels are usually lower; therefore, exterior obstructions of the sky dome are a disadvantage rather than an advantage, as they are in sunny clear skies. Sometimes, if the cloud cover is quite thin, the overcast sky can be very bright and a potential source of glare. Because the overcast sky is three times as bright at the zenith as it is at the horizon, adjacent facades that

Court Window   Dubai

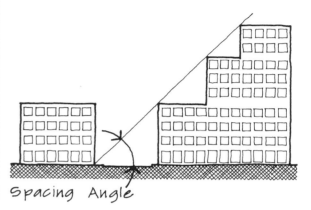

Spacing Angle

Climate	Latitude	Minimum Spacing Angle
warm humid	0 - 10°	40°
composite	15°	45°
composite/desert	20°	50°
desert	25°	50°
mediterranean/ desert	30°	45°
mediterranean	35°	40°
mediterranean/ temperate	40°	35°
temperate	45°	30°
temperate	50°	25°
cold temperate	60°	22°

Daylight Access Spacing Angles for Different Latitudes

are tall and close obstruct more of the upper sky dome than those smaller or further away. Therefore, street and court width and facade reflectivity become the primary determinants of how much light is available to the street itself.

The chart indicates spacing angles recommended for residential building types. They assume overcast sky conditions typical of the latitudes listed, daylight factors adequate for residential tasks, and continuous building rows (M. Evans, p. 74).

The relationships between sky type, latitude, surface reflectivity, building spacing and continuity, and building shape and height are complex and the spacing angles in the table may be more restrictive than necessary under many circumstances. Actual site situations may be predicted more accurately using methods proposed in Hopkinson et al., Ch. 17, "Daylight and Design-Town Planning," or *Midtown Development,* Department of City Planning (New York), p. 61, "Zoning: Bulk Regulations."

Mashrabiyya

STREETS, OPEN SPACES, AND BUILDINGS:
Orientation and Location

22. *Favorable microclimates created by topography can be used to locate building groups. [heating and cooling]*

On a large scale, topography, solar radiation and wind combine to produce microclimates that accentuate certain characteristics of the macroclimate of the area. These microclimates make some locations within the topography more desirable than others, depending on the macroclimate.

These considerations are much more important for exterior spaces or skin-load–dominated buildings, in which heating and cooling loads are affected primarily by climate, than for internal-load–dominated buildings in which heating and cooling requirements are affected primarily by how much heat is generated in the building and which have a cooling requirement much of the time.

The general design objectives for each climatic region are:

- Cold—Maximize the warming effects of solar radiation. Reduce the impact of winter wind.
- Temperate—Maximize warming effects of the sun in winter. Maximize shade in summer. Reduce the impact of winter wind but allow air circulation in summer.
- Hot arid—Maximize shade and minimize wind.
- Hot humid—Maximize shade and wind.

As the diagramatic section shows, the most favorable microclimate location for each climate region is:

- Cold—*Low on a south-facing slope* to increase solar radiation; low enough to give wind protection but high enough to avoid cold air collection at the bottom of the valley
- Temperate—*In the middle to upper part* of the slope with access to both sun and wind but protection from high winds
- Hot arid—*At the bottom of the slope* for exposure to cold air flow at night and on east orientations for decreased solar exposure in the afternoons
- Hot humid—*At the top of the slope* for exposure to wind and on east orientations for decreased solar exposure in the afternoons (Robinette, 1977, p. 69; Zeren, p. 35)

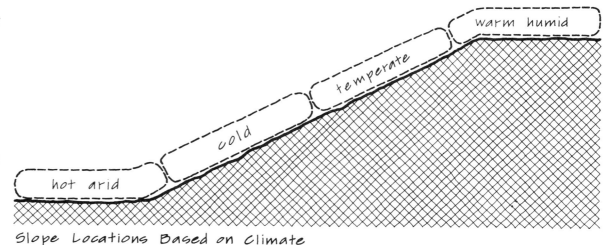

Slope Locations Based on Climate

OPEN SPACES AND BUILDINGS: Shape and Orientation

23. *Buildings can be located and arranged to form wind-protected, sunny exterior spaces.* **[heating]**

An outdoor space can be comfortable for a person with moderately warm clothing at temperatures as low as 40°F if the wind is blocked and sufficient solar radiation is available (see Climate as a Context, Technique 10). Comfort can also be achieved at lower temperatures, depending on the insulation provided by heavier clothing or on more strenuous activity levels.

Sun in open spaces and shading from the buildings that form the open space can easily be evaluated using a model and the sundials from Climate as a Context, Technique 1.

In the absence of precise information from wind tunnel simulations, one could expect, as a rule of thumb, that the area of *reduced wind velocity on the leeward side of the building group should extend to at least three to four times the building height* (Melaragno, pp. 347, 377). Based on studies of wind breaks, *the reduction in velocity will be at the most 75 to 80%* near the building, decreasing as one moves to the leeward.

Ralph Erskine's town project in Resolute Bay, Canada, illustrates the potential impact of this design strategy. This new town is located halfway up a south-facing slope to maximize its exposure to the sun, while avoiding the high wind velocities characteristic of the hill tops. The complex is organized as a "sun trap," with the tallest buildings at the north, where they provide protection from the prevailing northwest wind and do not shade outdoor spaces. The dwellings, school, and circulation routes are placed within this sun trap, maximizing the microclimatic comfort while allowing the city's inhabitants to maintain contact with the outside environment in going about their daily tasks (*Architectural Design*, Vol. 11; Vol 12, No. 11, No. 12, 1977).

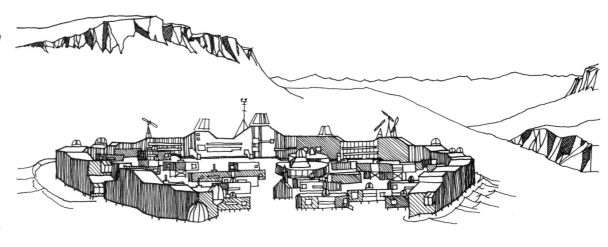

Town Project Resolute Bay   R. Erskine

24. *Wind breaks can be used to create edges that shelter buildings and open spaces.* [heating and cooling]

Windbreaks can be used to protect both buildings and outside areas from hot and cold winds. In cold climates wind breaks can reduce the heat loss in buildings by reducing wind flow over the buildings, thereby reducing infiltration and convection losses. If the wind is blocked in outside areas that have access to sun, people can be comfortable at temperatures as low as 45° (see Technique 10).

When the winds to be blocked come from a prevailing direction, partial wind screens like the L-shaped ones sheltering clusters of farm buildings in **Shiman Prefecture in Western Japan** can be used. When winds are more varied, a more completely enclosing shelter may be required. On the Italian island of **Pantelleria**, stone walls completely surround single lemon trees to protect them from the wind.

When trees are used as barriers, the velocity reduction behind the windbreak depends on their height, density, cross-sectional shape, width, and length. Height and density are the most important factors. *Reductions in wind speeds of 62 to 78% occur in an area five times the barrier height on the lee side of a moderately dense wind break, 24 to 62% in the area five to ten barrier heights, and 13 to 23% in the area ten to fifteen barrier heights beyond the wind break* (R.A. Reed, p. 5). When the wind doesn't blow perpendicular to the windbreak, the area of reduced velocity is decreased.

In hot dry climates, in addition to thermal comfort, walls provide important dust and sand protection. Because of their light weight,

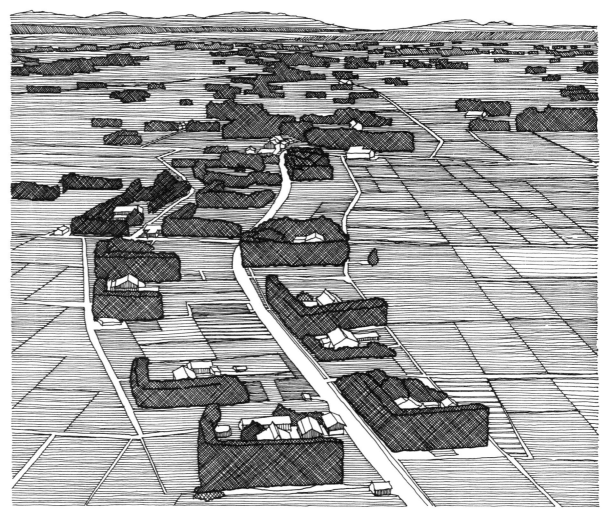

Shimane Prefecture Western Japan

dust particles follow the main air stream around the building, so eddy areas of reduced velocity formed by courts and walls are less dusty. *Courts that are at most two times longer than the building height offer good dust protection. Walls on the windward side should be as high as the building and less than 20' from the building. Sand, because it is heavier, can be stopped with lower walls, down to a height of 5'6"* (Saini, 1980, p. 60).

The wind reduction from *fences* depends on their porosity and their height. *The maximum reduction occurs in an area 2 to 7 times the barrier height on the leeward side of the barrier* for a wind blowing perpendicular to the barrier. *A barrier of 36% permeability shows a reduction of 90% at four times the barrier height, 70% at eight times, 30% at sixteen times, and 5% at thirty-two times the barrier height* (Melaragno, p. 377).

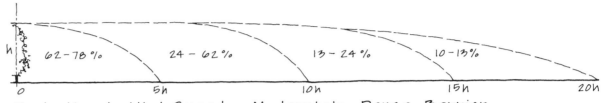

Reduction in Wind Speed - Moderately Dense Barrier

Giardino in Pantelleria

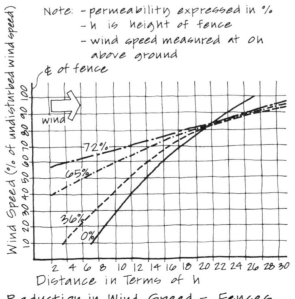

Note: - permeability expressed in %
- h is height of fence
- wind speed measured at 0h above ground

Reduction in Wind Speed - Fences

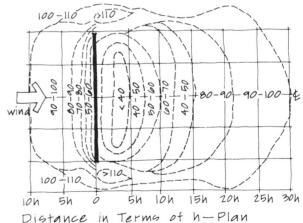

Distance in Terms of h—Plan
- wind speed percentage of unobstructed wind
- h is height of windbreak

Distribution of Velocity Around a Moderately Dense Windbreak

OPEN SPACES AND BUILDINGS: Edges

25. *Edges of water can be formed to cool incoming breezes. [cooling]*

In hot arid climates, water evaporating into the air can substantially reduce the air temperature. The evaporation rate and therefore the cooling rate depends upon the area of the water, the velocity of the wind, the relative humidity of the air, and the water temperature. Of these, the designer has the most control over the area of water and its location relative to the spaces to be cooled. In addition to increasing the surface area of the pond, the effective area can be increased by sprays in pools or on other surfaces. The cooling effect can be localized in courts that trap the cool air or used in larger areas to cool the air flowing through the building. Frank Lloyd Wright used fountains in protected areas to provide a cool oasis from the hot desert air and pools to cool the air moving through the building at **Taliesin West** near Phoenix, Arizona (Hitchcock, 1942, Illus. 357).

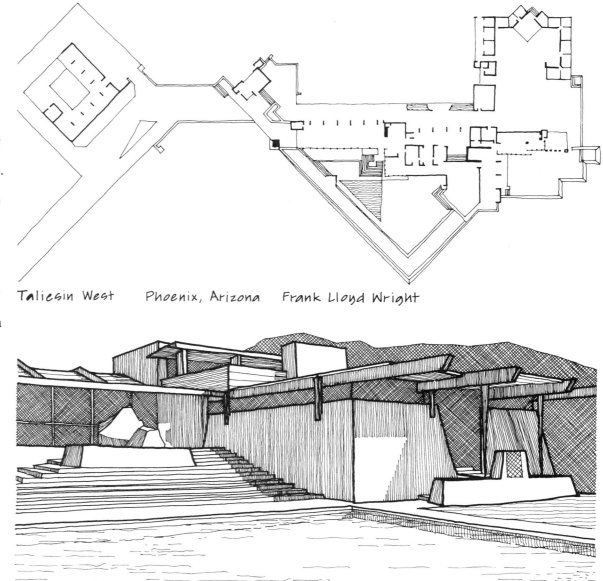

Taliesin West   Phoenix, Arizona   Frank Lloyd Wright

Taliesin West   Phoenix, Arizona   Frank Lloyd Wright

OPEN SPACES AND BUILDINGS:
Dispersed Organizations

26. *Buildings and open spaces can be organized to preserve each building's access to breezes. [cooling]*

Each building creates an area of reduced wind velocity on its leeward side; therefore, buildings in which *cross-ventilation is important should be separated by a distance of five to seven times the building height to assure adequate airflow* if they are directly behind one another (M. Evans, p. 64; Koenigsberger et al., p. 129). Compared to multistory buildings, lower one-story buildings cause smaller wind shadows and can be spaced close together, as they are in the village of **Tocamacho,** on the Mosquito Coast of Honduras. If the buildings are staggered, the windflow around one building helps provide ventilation air for the adjacent building and the spacing may be decreased.

Tocamacho   Mosquito Coast   Honduras

OPEN SPACES AND BUILDINGS:
Elongated Organizations

27. *Building groups can be elongated in the east–west direction and spaced in the north–south direction to insure solar gain to each building. [heating]*

The placement of a building such that it has access to the sun without shading other buildings has important implications for the form and arrangement of groups of buildings.

Individual dwelling units at **Pueblo Acoma,** in New Mexico, are arranged in long, thin east–west enlongated clusters, each having a south-facing terrace. The clusters of dwellings are spaced far enough apart in the north–south direction that even in the winter, when sun angles are low, the higher buildings do not shade their neighbors to the north (Knowles, 1974, p. 27).

Tony Garnier's plan for an ideal city, **"Cite Industrielle,"** was similar to Pueblo Acoma in its concern for south orientation and shading; he developed blocks elongated east–west to maximize the south-facing frontage and located individual dwellings on their lots so that they did not shade adjacent buildings (Butti & Perlin, p. 164).

The appropriate spacing between buildings is determined by the low altitude of the winter sun. The sun angle chart is based on the sun position on December 21 for eight Northern Hemisphere latitudes. *Multiply the height of the building, H, by the value X from the table to determine the spacing, S, that will provide optimum winter exposure* for a cluster of buildings.

This optimization will change substantially if the site is sloped. The spacing must increase for north-facing slopes and decrease for south-facing slopes, as can be seen in Atelier 5's **Siedlung Halen,** in Bern, Switzerland. The northern units are much closer to

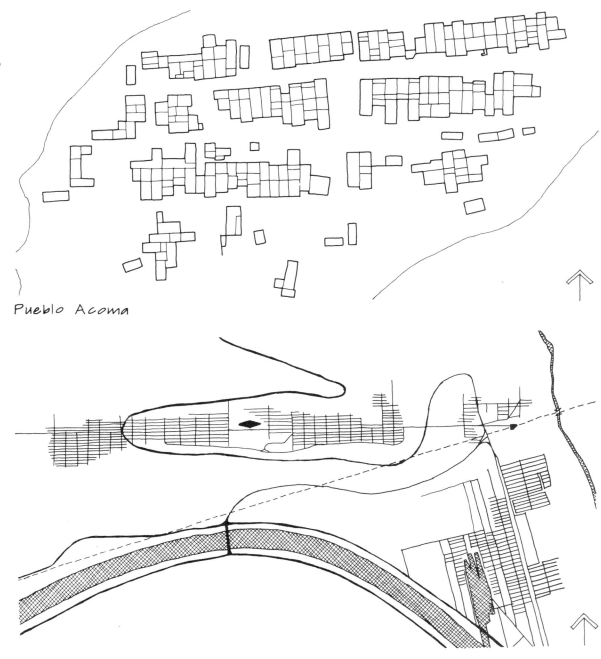

Pueblo Acoma

Cité Industrielle   Tony Garnier

the southern units than they could be on a
flat site, thereby allowing a more compact development of the site without sacrificing
southern exposure (Global Architecture, Vol.
5).

Values of x
December 21

Latitude	9am	10am	11am	noon	1pm	2pm	3pm
24° N.	1.4	1.2	1.1	1.1	1.1	1.2	1.4
28° N.	1.7	1.4	1.3	1.3	1.3	1.4	1.7
32° N.	2.1	1.7	1.5	1.5	1.5	1.7	2.1
36° N.	2.5	2.1	1.8	1.7	1.8	2.1	2.5
40° N.	3.1	2.4	2.2	2.1	2.2	2.4	3.1
44° N.	4.0	2.9	2.6	2.5	2.6	2.9	4.0
52° N.	5.7	3.7	3.3	3.1	3.3	3.7	5.7
	9.5	5.1	4.3	4.0	4.3	5.1	9.5

$s = xh$

h, building height

s, spacing

Building Spacing

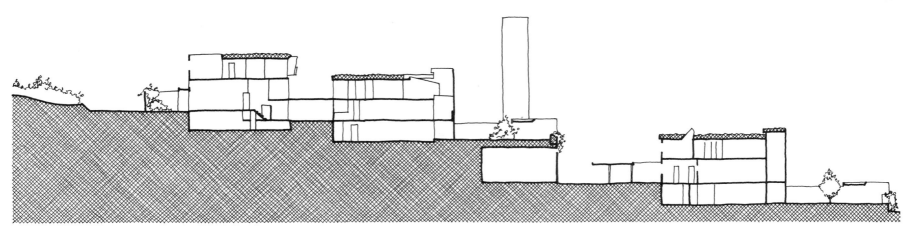

Siedlung Halen   Bern, Switzerland   Atelier 5

OPEN SPACES AND BUILDINGS:
Compact Organizations

28. *Buildings can be arranged to shade each other and adjacent exterior spaces.* *[cooling]*

Buildings that have a cooling load because of their high internal heat gain may be easier to shade than buildings whose cooling load is caused primarily by climate. Buildings that have a high rate of internal gain frequently require shading in the winter and can be effectively shaded by their neighbors to the south when the sun is low in the sky.

When shading is required in the summer or at low latitudes, buildings are difficult to use as shading devices for each other because the sun is high, casting short shadows except in the early morning and late afternoon.

In hot arid climates, which do not rely on cross-ventilation cooling strategies, buildings are placed very close together, as they are in **Marrakech, Morocco,** in order to shade each other and adjacent streets.

When the sun is high, horizontal shading elements like roofs or tree canopies are extremely effective, especially in hot humid climates where buildings are placed further apart to encourage cross-ventilation.

The sun's movement throughout the year can be simulated, and the effectiveness of shading can be most easily be evaluated using a model and sundial as described in Climate as a Context, Technique 1.

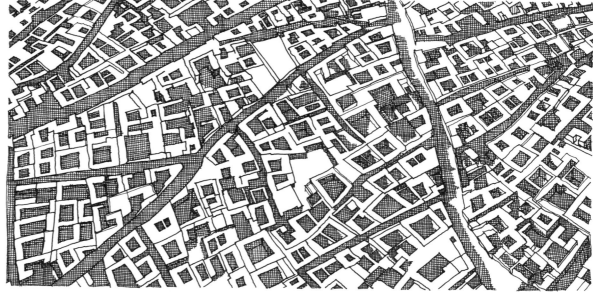

Marrakesh, Morocco

OPEN SPACES AND BUILDINGS:
Interwoven Organizations

29. *Interwoven organizations of buildings and planting can be used to reduce the ambient air temperature. [cooling]*

The temperature in densely built-up areas is frequently several degrees higher than in the surrounding rural areas due to heat generation from fuels, increased absorption and storage of solar radiation, and reduced wind speed due to surface roughness.

Planted areas can be as much as 10 to 15°F lower than built-up areas due to a combination of evapotranspiration, reflection, shading, and storage of cold.

Planted areas, like the palm groves surrounding and intersecting the town of **Oatif, Al Hasa, Saudi Arabia,** can be used as sources of cooler air that is drawn into the built-up areas as the hot air in those areas rises. Hypothetical studies suggest that for a city of one million (Myrup, p. 918), *urban temperatures do not start decreasing until the evaporating surfaces, i.e., planting, are 10 to 20% of the city area. The minimum air temperature decreases by 6 to 7°F, and the maximum temperature decreases from 9 to 10°F as the evaporating area goes from 20 to 50% of the city.*

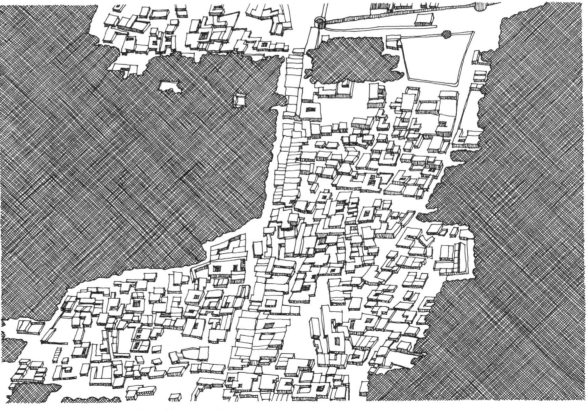

Qatif, Al Hasa, Saudi Arabia

B

Buildings

The strategies at the buiilding scale deal with single buildings and their major components, rooms and courtyards. This section contains more strategies than either of the other two scales, which probably reflects the importance of this scale in the schematic design stage and the fact that much of the research and testing has been done at the buiilding scale.

Strategies 31, 32, 48, 49, and 50 deal with the appropriate orientation of single rooms and organizations of rooms to the sun and wind. Strategies 33, 34, 35, 36, 37, 38, 40, and 43 concentrate on appropriate shapes of single rooms and groups of rooms. A few, Strategies 44, 45, 46, 47, and 51, suggest how activities and their associated rooms can be zoned in response to light, temperature variations, and sources of heat and cold. Two of the strategies (Strategies 30 and 46) discuss the protection of rooms from the extremes of heat and cold.

ROOMS: Edges

30. *Earth edges can be used to shelter buildings from extremes of heat and cold.* [heating and cooling]

Earth sheltering reduces heat loss and heat gain in two ways, by increasing the resistance to heat flow of the walls, roof, and floor, and by reducing the temperature difference between inside and out. At a depth greater than two feet below the earth's surface, daily temperature fluctuations are negligible. The annual average earth temperature ranges from 45°F in the northern United States to 75°F in the Florida peninsula. This temperature may be estimated from the map of shallow well temperatures. The annual temperature range variation around this average depends on depth: ± 13°F at 4 feet, ±8°F at 8 feet, and ±5°F at 12 feet (Watson & Labs, p. 104).

To estimate the temperature difference, ΔT, between inside and outside, which you must know to calculate heat loss, adjust the average annual earth temperature by the annual temperature variation at the depth being considered. When calculating heat loss, remember that the ground temperature peak lags behind surface earth temperature by 10 to 13 weeks (Labs, p. 129).

The heat resistance of an earth-sheltered wall (not including the wall itself) at a given depth may be estimated from the graph. Enter the graph on the left side of the horizontal axis with the depth below the top of the berm or grade. Then move vertically to the family of diagonal lines representing berm types, then horizontally until intersecting the soil type diagonal line. Finally, move down to the horizontal axis to determine the R-value of the wall at that depth. Calculate the average of the R-values at the top and bottom of the

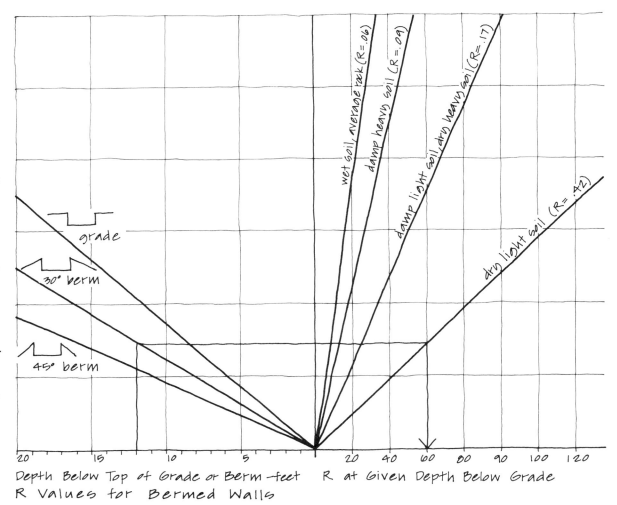

Depth Below Top of Grade or Berm —feet   R at Given Depth Below Grade

R Values for Bermed Walls

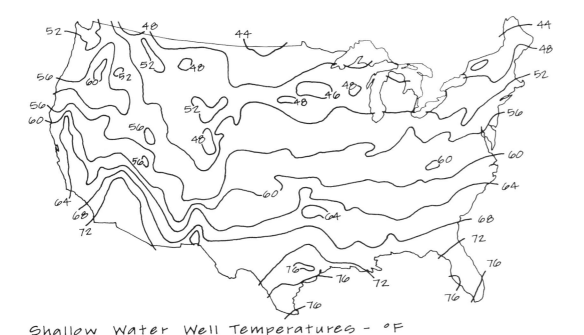

Shallow Water Well Temperatures - °F

	completely covered	walls covered	partly covered
sinking			
berming			

Types of Earth Sheltering

wall, or find the R at some representative intermediate depth to determine the wall's average R-value.

Earth sheltering takes two basic forms, either sinking the building into the excavated earth or berming the earth up around the building on grade. In both forms, earth sheltering may range from partially covered walls to totally covered walls to completely covered walls and roof.

In the **Cooperative Homesteads** project, Detroit, 1942, and the **Jacobs II** house, Frank Lloyd Wright used berms formed with earth from sunken gardens to protect the buildings from winter winds and provide insulation (Sergeant, pp. 76, 82). The Jacobs house is a classic example of a house tuned to the cold Wisconsin climate, reducing the loss of heat on the north with the berm, while opening the south wall and garden to the warming sun.

The **Winston House** in New Hampshire by Don Metz (*Architectural Record*, 5/74, p. 52) is similar to the Jacobs II house with its closed north and open south. However, it is built into

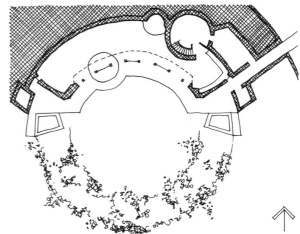

Jacobs II House Middleton, Wisconsin
F. L. Wright

a hillside, and the earth completely covers the roof.

The **Bookstore at the University of Minnesota** by Meyers and Bennett (*Progressive Architecture*, 1/75, p. 52) was completely buried in the earth to increase its energy efficiency and maintain the openness of that section of the campus.

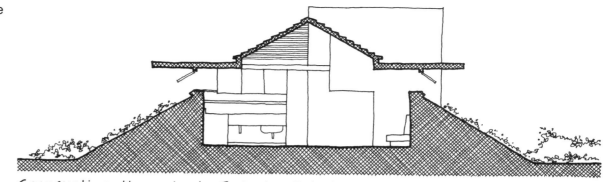

Cooperative Homesteads Project   Detroit, Michigan   Frank Lloyd Wright

Winston House   Lyme, New Hampshire   Don Metz

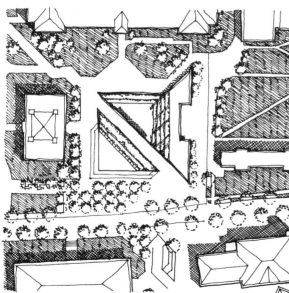

East Bank Bookstore   University of Minnesota
Myers & Bennett Architects

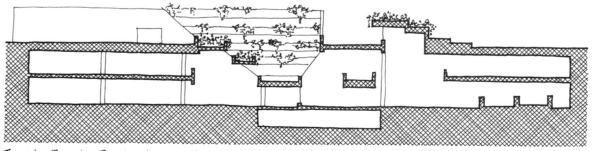

East Bank Bookstore   University of Minnesota
Myers & Bennett Architects

ROOMS: Orientation

31. *The vertical glazing on solar-heated spaces should be no more than 20° to 30° from true south. [heating]*

In the winter months when the sky is clear and the sun is low, the most radiation falls on a south-facing surface, because radiation is most intense at noon and decreases rapidly several hours before and after. In addition, the amount of radiation reflected off the glazing increases as the angle between the glazing and the sun's rays increases (ASHRAE, p. 394). Local climatic conditions that produce morning or afternoon cloudiness can change the optimum true south orientation slightly. Also, because the heat gained in the afternoon can be more effectively stored for use at night, solar-heated buildings frequently perform best if oriented a few degrees west of south. *If the glazing is within 20° east of south and 30° west of south, the decrease in performance will be less than 10% of the optimum* (Balcomb, Barley, et al, p. 28).

Frank Lloyd Wright used this flexibility in orientation to bend the rooms in the **Marting House** in a semi-circle to form a south-facing outside terrace (*Architectural Forum*, Jan. 1948).

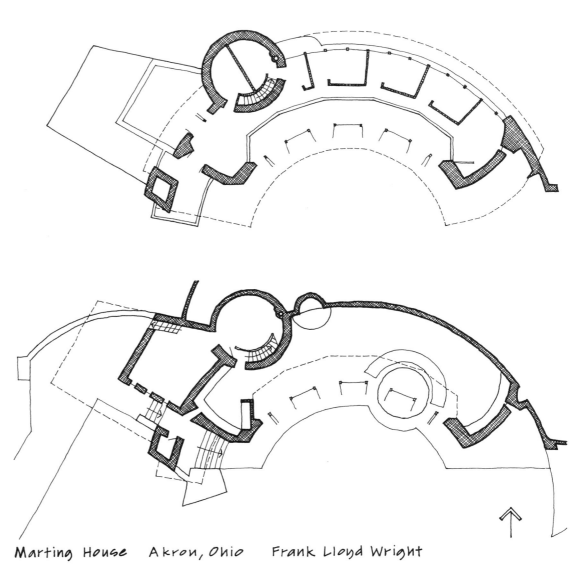

Marting House   Akron, Ohio   Frank Lloyd Wright

32. *Rooms oriented to the prevailing breeze increase the effectiveness of cross-ventilation. [cooling]*

The rate at which air flows through a room, carrying heat with it, is a function of the area of the inlets and outlets, the wind speed, the direction of the wind relative to the openings, and the temperature difference between inside and outside the building. As air flows around a building, it causes higher pressure zones on the windward side and lower pressure zones in the lee of the building. The most effective cross-ventilation occurs when the inlets are placed in the higher pressure area and the outlets in the lower pressure zones. The rate of air flow depends on the pressure difference between inlet and outlet (Melarango, p. 32l). The maximum rate of ventilation occurs when the area of the inlets and outlets is large and the wind is perpendicular to the window openings.

The maximum ventilating area may be achieved as in Paul Rudolph's **house in Sarasota, Florida,** by treating almost the entire house as a single room and opening its opposite walls completely with operable louvers (Fry & Drew, p. 75).

A **church in the Philippines** adopts a similar strategy, completely opening its long sides with folding doors. All the ventilating openings are protected with deep overhangs or interior drains so that the building may be ventilated during rain storms (Fry & Drew, p. 181).

Effective ventilation may be achieved when the wind does not come from a direction perpendicular to the window (Givoni, p. 289). *Variations in orientation up to 30° from perpendicular to the prevailing wind do not significantly reduce ventilation.*

When openings cannot be oriented to the prevailing breeze, landscaping can be used to

Cacoon House   Sarasota, Florida   Paul Rudolph

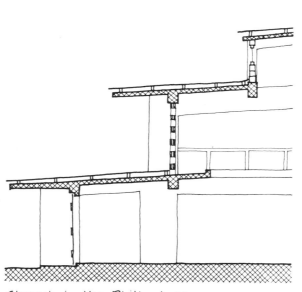

Church in the Philippines

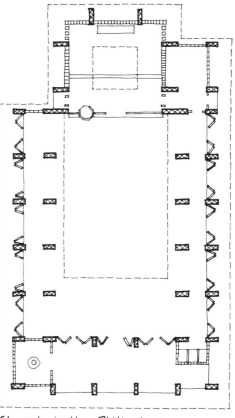

Church in the Philippines

alter the positive and negative pressure zones around the building and induce wind flow through windows parallel to the prevailing wind directions (R.H. Reed, p. 56; Robinette, 1977, p. 29).

The size of the opening required to remove internally generated heat, as a percentage of floor area, assuming a difference of 3°F between inside and out, may be determined from the graph. Enter the graph on the vertical axis with the wind speed, move horizontally until the heat gain curves are intersected; then drop down to the horizontal axis to read the size of the inlet (and outlet) as a percentage of the floor area. See Climate as a Context (Techniques 4 and 5) for wind analysis, Program and Use (Techniques 11, 12, and 13) and Form and Envelope (Technique 15) for heat gain analysis, or Combining Climate, Program and Form (Technique 18). If the temperature difference between inside and out is less than 3°F, the openings need to be proportionally larger, and if the temperature difference is greater, the openings may be smaller. Because occupant cooling is a function of air movement as well as heat removal, when the temperature is above the comfort zone, openings may need to be sized on the basis of maintaining a certain wind velocity through the building. (See Windows: Location and Orientation, Strategy 64.)

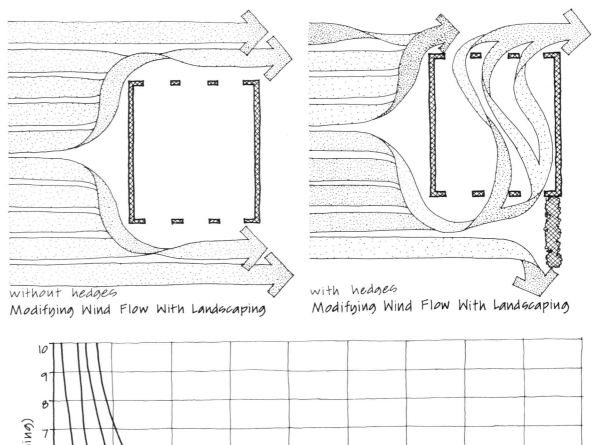

without hedges
Modifying Wind Flow With Landscaping

with hedges
Modifying Wind Flow With Landscaping

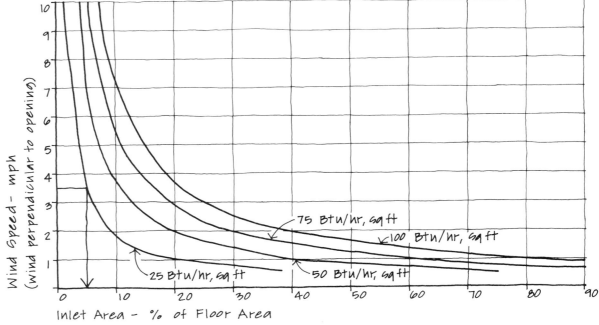

Cross Ventilation — Required Inlet Area

ROOMS: Shape and Enclosure

33. *Rooms that are open to collect the sun can store heat within the space. [heating]*

The proportion of the annual heating load that can be supplied by the sun results from a delicate balance between the amount of collectible solar radiation, the amount of heat loss, and the amount of heat that can be stored during the day for use at night. Collectible radiation is a function of the amount of south-facing glazing and available radiation; the amount of heat loss is a function of the insulating qualities of the building skin and the severity of the climate.

Direct gain solar systems collect radiation in habitable spaces to heat the air and thermal mass. The thermal mass absorbs the heat, which keeps the air temperature from rising too high during the day and gives its stored heat back to the space at night (Mazria, p. 28).

As the amounts of south-facing glazing and thermal mass increase, greater demands are placed on the shape, orientation, and materials of rooms.

The **Shelton Solar Cabin,** by James Lambeth, is a diagrammatic expression of these demands. The south exposure of the cabins is enlarged in both plan and section and filled with glass, while the remaining exposures are reduced in size, almost windowless, and well-insulated. The concrete floor is used for thermal storage (Lambeth & Delap, p. 56).

The **Milford Reservation Solar Conservation Center,** by Kelbaugh and Lee, uses a section similar to Lamberth's but at a larger scale and with its largest wall facing north rather than south. This gave the architects the opportunity to puncture the roof with dormers, thereby increasing the south-facing glazing area and allowing sunlight to penetrate to the north

edge of the building (*Progressive Architecture*, 4/80, p. 16; 4/81, p. 118).

The **Mere House,** a superlative design by the outstanding design group Bumpzoid, increases the southern exposure of its major room by elongating it in the east–west direction without sacrificing the room's important axial connection to the lake on the east end.

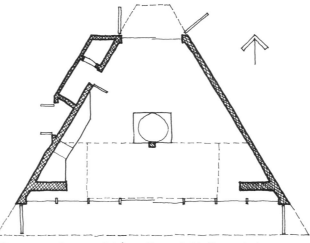

Shelton Solar Cabin Hazel Valley, Arkansas James Lambeth

Shelton Solar Cabin Hazel Valley, Arkansas James Lambeth

The masonry stairway that runs the length of the south wall serves as a place for heat storage (*Architectural Record*, May 1983, p. 90).

The recommended amount of south-facing glazing, as a percentage of floor area, can be estimated by taking the value from the map for your location and multiplying it by the value from the Geometry Factors table that

Milford Reservation Environmental Center Milford, Pennsylvania Kelbaugh & Lee

corresponds to the floor area of your building. The amount of glazing you choose should be within 20% of the estimated value. These values are based on balancing the cost of conservation strategies, like insulating, against the cost of solar gain, that is, windows and mass. They are based on current fuel costs and tend to predict small glazing areas. See Windows: Size, Strategy 60, for more detailed sizing information. The estimate applies to direct gain, trombe walls, sunspaces, and combinations of these. The values in the tables are applicable to residential or small commercial buildings with internal heat gains of 30 to 60 Btu per sq. ft. per day, that are well insulated and have low infiltration and ventilation rates. The values on the map are equal to 1/(load collector ratio) (conservation factor) (Balcomb, 1983, p. 117).

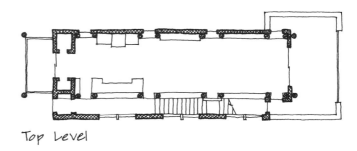

Top Level

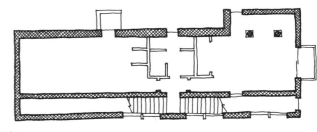

Middle Level

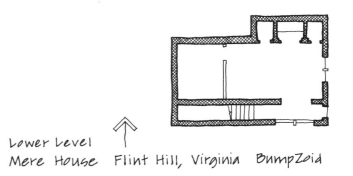

Lower Level

Mere House   Flint Hill, Virginia   BumpZoid

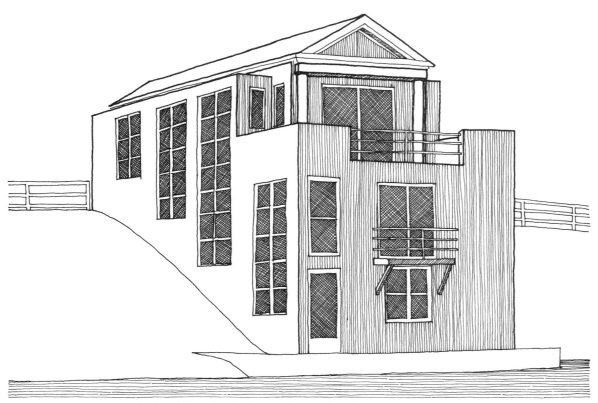

Mere House   Flint Hill, Virginia   BumpZoid

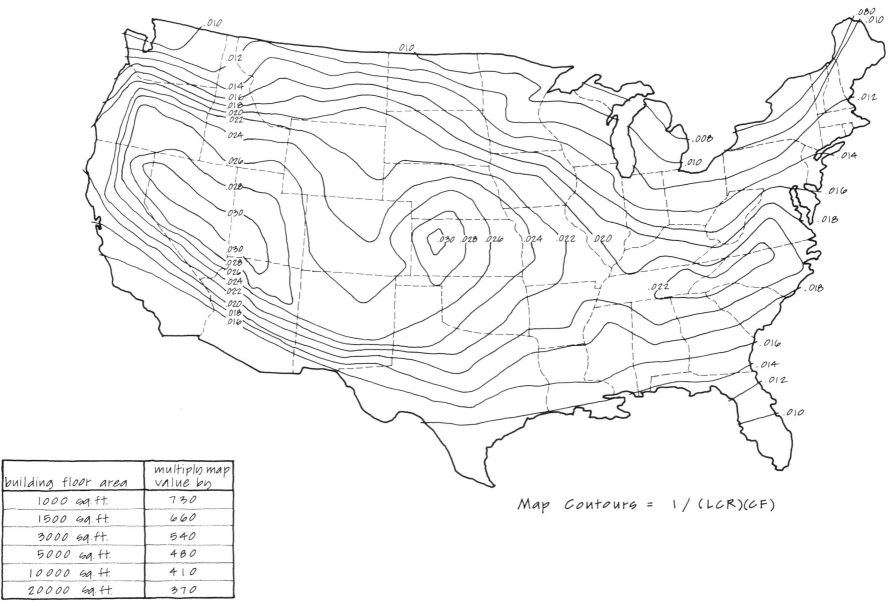

building floor area	multiply map value by
1000 sq. ft.	730
1500 sq. ft.	660
3000 sq. ft.	540
5000 sq. ft.	480
10000 sq. ft.	410
20000 sq. ft.	370

Geometry Factors

Map Contours = 1 / (LCR)(CF)

ROOMS: Shape and Enclosure

34. *A sunspace can be used to collect the sun's heat and distribute it to other rooms. [heating]*

A sunspace, unlike direct gain and trombe wall systems, adds a room to the building. Since the purpose of the sunspace is to provide heat to the rest of the building, it experiences large diurnal temperature swings and is therefore not always comfortable. In sunny periods it will be too warm, and at night it will be too cold. It is usually assumed that the sunspace can get as hot as 95 °F and as cool as 45 °F. The sunspace may be attached to the main space, sharing one common wall, or enclosed within it, sharing three common walls. Heat is usually transferred to the main space through a common masonry thermal storage wall and by convection through openings in the common wall. The common wall may also be an insulated wall with all the mass located in the sunspace and the heat transfer completely dependent on thermocirculation.

In the **International Meeting Center** in West Berlin by Otto Steidle and Partner, the sunspaces are used as a buffer zone between inside and out, extending the living area and providing heat on sunny days. The projecting sunspaces visually break down the mass of the 80-unit apartment building, allowing it to be read as five separate houses, more to scale with other buildings in the neighborhood (*Progressive Architecture*, 4/81).

The area of sunspace glazing as a percentage of the building floor area can be estimated using the map in Rooms: Shape and Enclosure, Strategy 33.

International Meeting Center   West Berlin   Otto Steidle & Partner

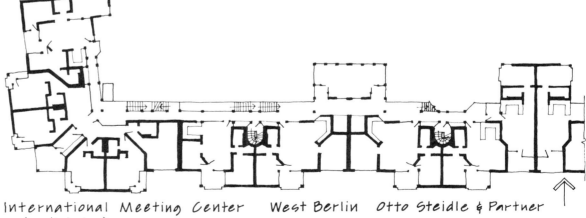

International Meeting Center   West Berlin   Otto Steidle & Partner
(partial plan)

35. *Solar heat can be collected and stored at the edge of the room. [heating]*

Indirect gain, or trombe wall, solar systems place the thermal storage mass between the space to be heated and the south-facing glazing. Consequently, unlike direct gain systems in their pure form, they do not allow sunlight into the heated space. The sun passes through the glazing and heats the thermal storage wall, which in turn heats the space. The rate of heat flow through the wall depends on the materials and thickness of the wall. In general, masonry storage walls delay the transfer of heat from the sunny side of the wall to the room by several hours. Water storage walls transfer the heat much more rapidly because they work by convection as well as conduction.

Unlike water walls, masonry storage walls can be used as bearing walls and because of their mass they make good acoustical barriers.

Two characteristics of trombe walls, their opaque, separating thickness and their creation of ambiguous areas of external glazing, are used effectively by Kelbaugh and Lee in the **Sisko house** in Metuchen, N.J. The trombe walls, which are interrupted by windows, provide an enclosing, well-defined, but nonoppressive edge for all the major rooms in the house. The south elevation makes a clear distinction between windows that are not in the trombe wall by articulating them on the facade and those that *are* part of the trombe wall by hiding them within the trombe wall glazing.

The area of trombe wall glazing, as a percentage of the building floor area, can be estimated using the map in Rooms: Shape and Enclosure, Strategy 33.

Sisko House   Metuchen, New Jersey   Kelbaugh & Lee

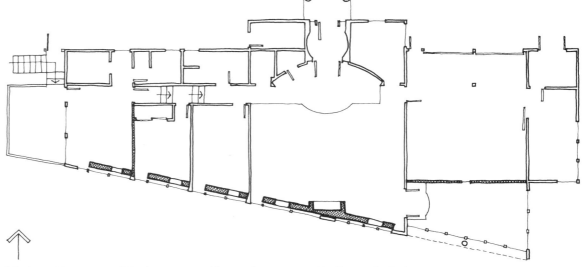

Sisko House   Metuchen, New Jersey   Kelbaugh & Lee

ROOMS: Shape and Enclosure

36. *Heat and cold can be collected and stored in the ceiling plane of the room.* [heating and cooling]

Roof ponds have the capacity for both heating and cooling and are particularly useful in the lower latitudes in buildings with both small heating and small cooling loads. They usually consist of water bags 4″ to 10″ deep, placed on a flat metal deck, the underside of which forms the ceiling surface, while its top surface is covered by movable insulation (Mazria, p. 194).

In the heating mode, the insulating panels slide open in the daytime, allowing the bags to collect and store solar heat. At night the insulating panels are closed, and the warm water and metal deck radiate their warmth to the room. In the cooling mode, the insulated panels are opened at night so that the bags radiate the heat they have stored from the day before to the night sky. During the day they are closed to protect the bags from the sun, and excess heat inside radiates and convects to the ceiling and is stored for release to the sky at night.

Heat absorption, especially in the higher latitudes, can be enhanced by reflectors. The cooling mode can be enhanced by wetting the bags so that night radiation is assisted by evaporative cooling. Heat transfer down from the ceiling can be significantly assisted by ceiling fans (Fleischnaker, Clark, & Giolma, p. 835).

The roof ponds are limited to one-story applications *with .5–1.0 sq. ft. of pond required for each square foot of floor area for buildings that generate internal heat gains similar to residences.* In climates with substantial cooling requirements, the necessary pond area usually approaches 100% of the floor area. As a result, storage of the movable insulation panels becomes an important consideration. This problem was solved in the **Sunstone house** in Phoenix, Arizona, designed by Daniel Arello, who put terraces on the east and north ends of the house, where the roofs form storage areas for the sliding insulating panel's (Wright & Andrejko, p. 127).

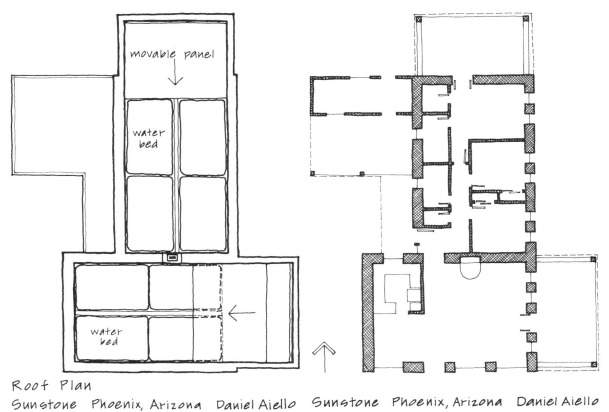

Roof Plan
Sunstone Phoenix, Arizona   Daniel Aiello   Sunstone Phoenix, Arizona   Daniel Aiello

37. Tall rooms with high and low openings increase the rate of stack ventilation. [cooling]

In a room cooled by stack ventilation, warm air rises, exits though openings at the top of the room, and is replaced by cooler air entering low in the room. The rate at which the air moves through the room, carrying heat with it, is a function of the vertical distance between the inlets and outlets, their size, and the difference between the outside temperature and the average inside temperature over the height of the room. Several strategies may be used to enhance this gravity ventilation system.

The effective height of the room can be increased by a stack at the top, as it is in this **Oregon hops drying barn.** The performance of the outlet may be enhanced, as in the **Pantheon,** regardless of wind direction, by placing it in a negative pressure or suction zone created by wind flowing over the building (Melaragno, p. 342). The room can be a large atrium, as it is in the **National Building Museum.** Outside air is drawn in through the small offices surrounding the atrium and exhausted through its top (Smith, p. 63).

Given the ventilation rate or the heat gain to be removed, use the graph to determine the height of the stack or room and the area of the inlets, which must be equaled or exceeded by the outlets, and the cross-section of the room or stack. This graph assumes a temperature difference of 3°F between inside and outside for other temperatures and unequally sized openings (ASHRAE, p. 344).

You can approximate heat gain by using the methods in Program and Use, Techniques 11, 12, and 13, and Form and Envelope, Technique 15, or Combining Climate, Program, and Form, Technique 18.

Oregon Hops Barn

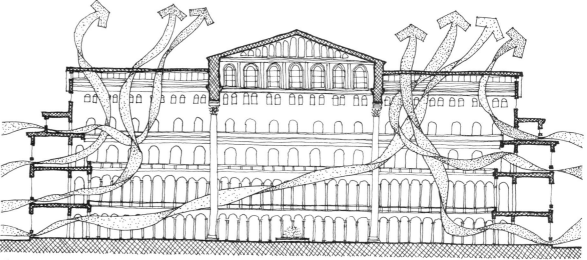

Pension Building   Washington, D.C.   Montgomery C. Meigs

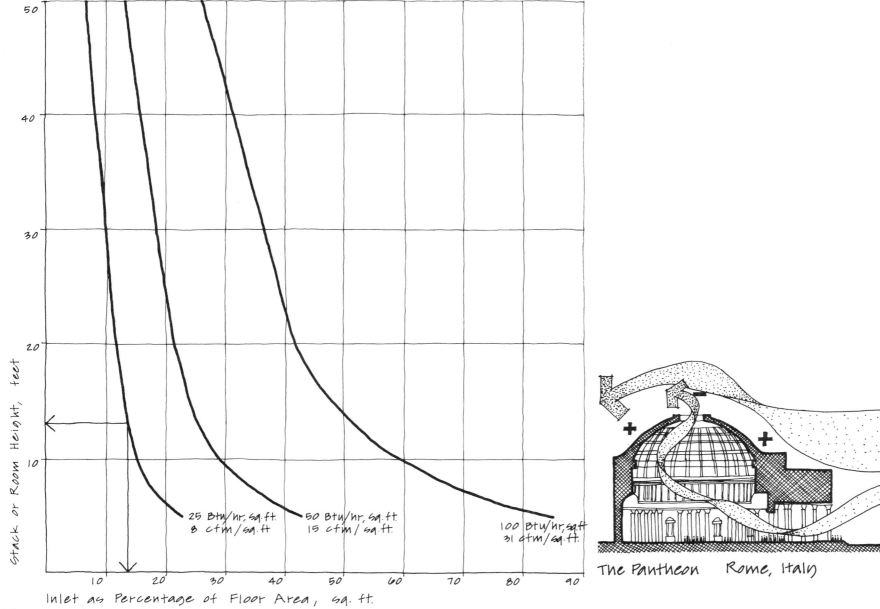

50

40

30

20

Stack or Room Height, feet

10

25 Btu/hr, sq. ft.   50 Btu/hr, sq. ft.
8 cfm/sq. ft   15 cfm/sq. ft.   100 Btu/hr, sq ft
                                             31 cfm/sq. ft.

10   20   30   40   50   60   70   80   90

Inlet as Percentage of Floor Area, sq. ft.

Stack   Ventilation

The Pantheon   Rome, Italy

ROOMS: Shape and Enclosure

38. ***The thermal mass in a room can be used to absorb heat from the room during the day and then be cooled at night with ventilation. [cooling]***

Cooling a building by the nighttime ventilation of the thermal mass depends upon a two-fold process. First, during the day, when the outside temperature is too warm for ventilation, any generated heat is stored in the building's mass. Second, at night, when the outside temperature is lower, outdoor air is allowed to ventilate through the building to remove its heat. The mass is thus cooled so that it can absorb excess heat again the next day. In order for this to work, there must be enough mass in the building to absorb the generated heat, and the mass must be distributed over enough surface area so that it will absorb the heat quickly and keep the interior air temperature comfortably low. The openings must be large to allow enough cool outside air to flow past the mass to remove the heat accumulated during the day and carry it outside the building.

The **Lane Energy Center** in Cottage Grove, Oregon, by Equinox Design, Inc., brings cool outside air into the building through an underground culvert running the length of the building. The culvert opens to the interior through floor vents. At night, as warm air is exhausted through wind-assisted stack ventilators at the high point of the roof, cool outside air is drawn into the building, flows over the floor mass, picks up heat, and rises towards the roof stacks.

In night ventilation schemes, the area of the mass that can be incorporated into a structure is a major limitation on the cooling potential of the scheme. The mass surface area is usually about 1 to 3 sq. ft. per square foot of floor because it is difficult to develop more

mass surface area within the building. (See Strategy 55). Therefore these rules of thumb are based on the area of mass that can be used for cooling, that is, exposed to night air movement, rather than on the internal heat generated.

To determine the area of inlet needed, which must be equalled by the outlet area and the cross-section of the stack, enter the graph on the vertical axis with wind speed for cross-ventilation or stack or room height for stack ventilation. Move horizontally until the appropriate curve is intersected; then drop down to determine the area of the inlet as a percentage of the mass area. The graph assumes that the wind blows from between perpendicular and diagonal to the openings for cross-ventilation and that the difference between the outside temperature and inside temperature is 3°F for stack ventilation (ASHRAE, p. 344).

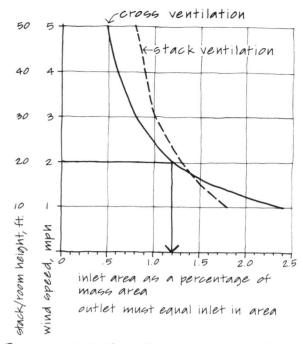

Percent of Cooling Mass Area in Inlet Area

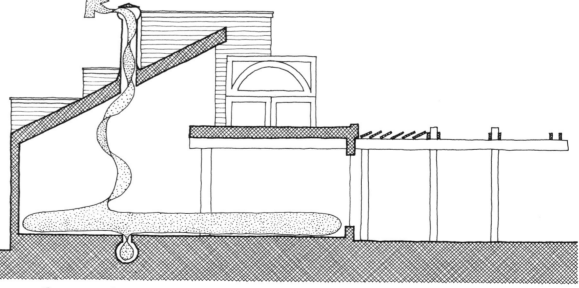

Lane Energy Center   Cottage Grove, Oregon   Equinox Design

ROOMS: Size

39. *The maximum room depth should be 2 to 2½ times the height of the window wall to maintain a minimum level of illumination and an even distribution of light. [daylighting]*

In a side-lit room the illumination is high near the window and falls off rapidly farther away from the window wall. The deeper the room, the greater the contrast between the area near the window and the wall furthest from the window. Under overcast conditions, assuming nearly continuous windows, when the room depth is greater than 2½ times the height of the window, the ratio between the brightest and darkest part of the room will exceed 5:1 (Flynn & Segil, p. 111). Excessive gradients tend to make the lighting seem uneven; and if the eye is adapted to the lightest parts of the room, especially the window, then the darker parts of the room will seem darker than they actually are (Hopkinson et al., p. 306).

The **Temple of Dendur wing at the Metropolitan Museum,** designed by Roche-Dinkeloo, is one large side-lit room whose light interior surfaces evenly distribute the light from the north-facing window, which runs from floor to ceiling and maximizes the amount of light entering the space.

As the room depth increases beyond 3 times the window wall height, the light levels in the darkest parts of the room approach 1% or less of the illumination available outside on an overcast day, which may be inadequate for some tasks. The light levels at the rear of the space will be greatly affected by reflectors at the window wall, the reflectivity of the interior surfaces and shading devices, and nonovercast sky conditions.

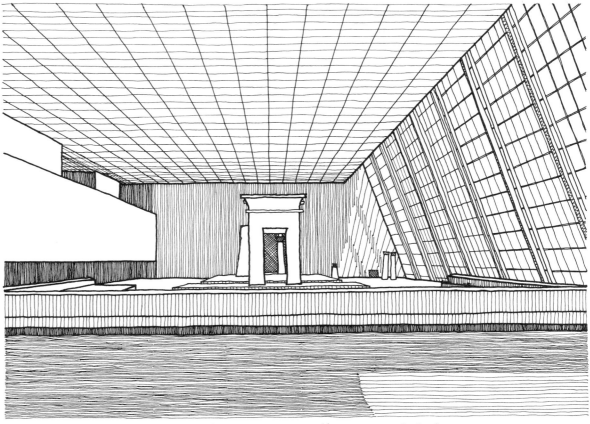

Temple of Dendur Wing   Metropolitan Museum of Art
New York City, New York   Roche & Dinkeloo

ROOMS: Thin Organizations

40. *Rooms organized into thin buildings will have daylight available for each space. [daylighting]*

The amount of light that reaches the interior of a room lit from one side is a function of the distance from the window, the height of the window above the floor, the size of the window, and the reflectivity of the room surfaces. As one moves away from the window wall, the proportion of the exterior daylight available inside decreases. Therefore, the width of the building is an important design consideration for a daylit building.

The **Wainwright Building** in St. Louis, Missouri, by Louis Sullivan, has side-lit offices arranged on both sides of a single corridor. The building is U-shaped to fit a corner site and to provide a continuous facade for both streets.

The "light courts" traditionally formed by O-, U-, and E-shaped buildings reduce the amount of light available to the windows that face them because the court walls absorb some of the light. Sullivan addressed this problem in the **Wainwright Building** by giving the rooms facing the court less depth than the ones facing the more open street.

The penetration of light into spaces can be enhanced by light shelves (see Building Parts and Windows: Layers, Strategy 65). It can also be reduced by roof overhangs (B. Evans, p. 62). When the sun is visible, either in the partly cloudy sky or the clear sky, the penetration of light into the space may be much greater than under overcast sky conditions. When sunlight reflectors are used, the width of the building may be greatly increased yet effectively daylit, as it was in the **TVA Building** (*AIA Journal*, 9/79).

Use the chart to determine the maximum room depth for a desired minimum daylight

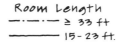

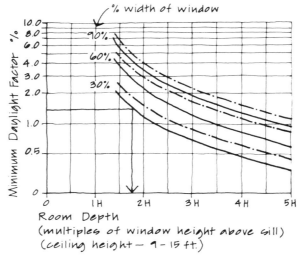

Minimum Daylight Factors—Unilateral Lighting

Wainwright Building
St. Louis, Missouri   Adler & Sullivan

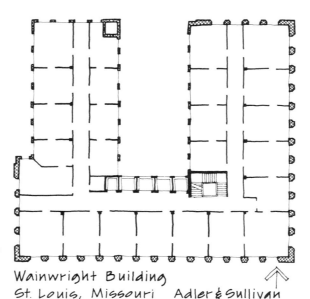

Wainwright Building   St. Louis, Missouri
Adler & Sullivan

factor two feet from the rear wall. *Enter the chart on the vertical axis at the desired daylight factor and proceed horizontally to the curve that corresponds to the ratio of window width to window wall width. Then move down to the horizontal axis that shows the maximum allowable room depth, in units of window height.* The graph assumes clear glazing, no external obstruction, reflectiveness of 70% in the ceiling, 50% in the walls, and 15% on the floor, a sill height of three feet, a head height one foot below the ceiling, and evenly distributed windows (CIE, p. 22).

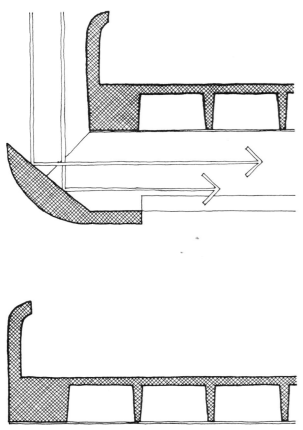

TVA Office Building
Chattanooga, Tennessee

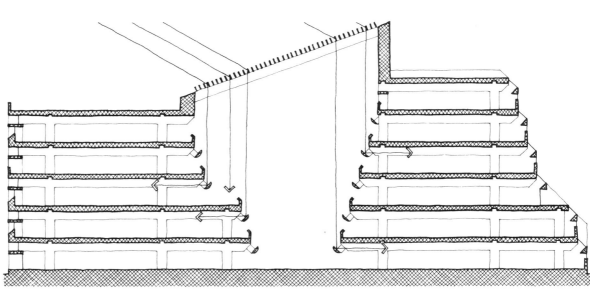

TVA Office Building   Chattanooga, Tennessee

ROOMS: Thin Organizations

41. *Rooms can be arranged along an east-west axis to increase south-facing skin available to collect solar radiation. [heating]*

As the proportion of south-facing glazing required in individual rooms for solar heating increases, so grows the necessity for care in organizing rooms with buildings, in both plan and section (see Rooms: Shape and Enclosure, Strategy 35 for glazing amounts).

The amount of south-facing skin, and thus the opportunity for south-facing glazing, may be increased by organizing the rooms along a south-facing circulation spine as it is in the **Hawkweed Group office** building in Osseo, Wisconsin (*Progressive Architecture,* 4/82, p. 132).

In the **Prince residence** designed by Equinox Design Inc., in Portland, Oregon, the circulation zone is a sunspace in some places and a direct gain space in others. It extends the full length of the south facade, organizing the living spaces along an east–west axis, so that each space has access to the sun's warmth and the view to the mountain range to the north.

Frank Lloyd Wright's Lewis House in Libertyville, Illinois, is also organized on an east-west axis, but with the circulation on the north, with all the rooms opening to the view of the river and the south sun.

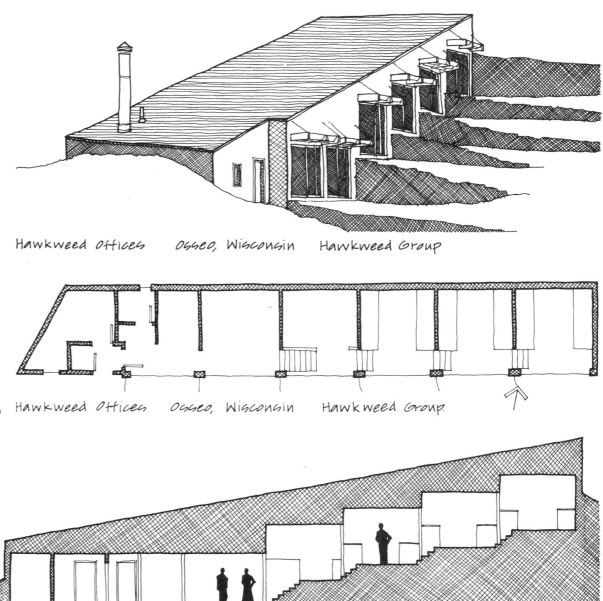

Hawkweed Offices   Osseo, Wisconsin   Hawkweed Group

Hawkweed Offices   Osseo, Wisconsin   Hawkweed Group

Hawkweed Offices   Osseo, Wisconsin   Hawkweed Group

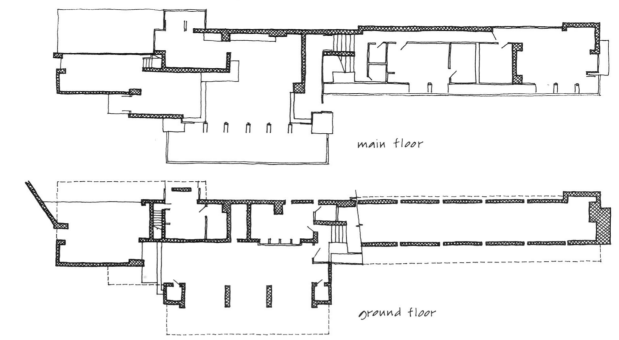

main floor

ground floor

Lloyd Lewis House   Libertyville, Illinois   F. L. Wright

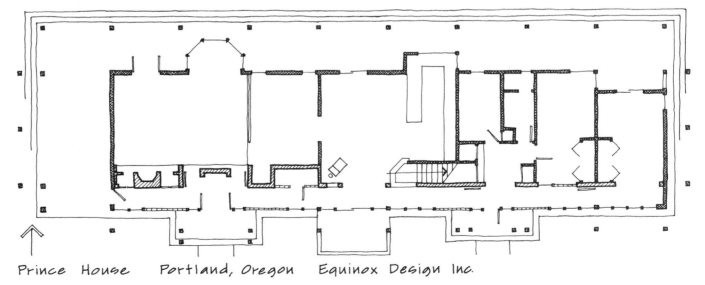

Prince House   Portland, Oregon   Equinox Design Inc.

ROOMS: Compact Organizations

42. *Rooms can be clustered to reduce skin area and heat loss and gain. [heating and cooling]*

The amount of exposed skin relative to the volume enclosed increases as compact forms like cubes elongate to forms like rectangles. Therefore the heat loss or gain through the skin by conduction and convection is greater for elongated forms than for compact forms of the same volume. When controlling heat loss or gain through the skin is a primary concern, rooms can be contracted into a compact form, as they were in the traditional **New England Salt Box,** in which case they also surrounded a central heat source. When this house fronts the south, it has the largest and the most windows facing south to collect the sun, and the source of constant heat, the kitchen, is on the coldest north side (Rifkind, p. 7).

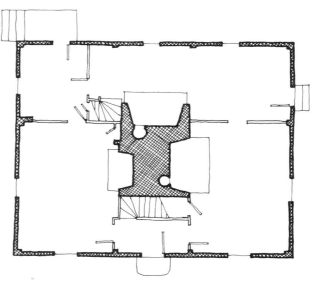

Old Ogden House   Fairfield, Conn.

Old Ogden House   Fairfield, Conn.   Old Ogden House   Fairfield, Conn.

ROOMS: Compact Organizations

43. Rooms can be organized to use both cross-ventilation and stack-ventilation. [cooling]

Cross-ventilation is a particularly valuable means of cooling during warm periods because it not only removes heat from the space but also increases the sensation of cooling by increasing people's rate of evaporation. However, in hot climates and in temperate climates at night, air movement is frequently slow, in which case stack ventilation becomes an important supplementary strategy. When choosing between stack- or cross-ventilation schemes, there is a conflict about how to design room organization. Linked room arrangements work well for cross-ventilation because each space can present a large part of its skin area to the prevailing breeze. On the other hand, bunched arrangements allow all the rooms to share the same ventilating stack. (See the design strategies for cross-ventilation, Strategy 32, and stack-ventilation, Strategy 37, for a more detailed explanation.)

The **Logan house** in Tampa, Florida, designed by Rowe Holmes Associates, resolved this dilemma by bunching the rooms to use a central stack but opens the three center spaces to each other and the outside to form a cross-ventilated breezeway through the entire house (*Progressive Architecture*, 6/81, p. 86).

If the openings are such that the flow rates for cross- and stack-ventilation can be coordinated, and if the flow rates are about the same for each, then the combined effect will be at its maximum at about 10% greater than could be achieved by either cross- or stack-ventilation acting alone. The percentage decreases rapidly as one flow rate predominates over the other (ASHRAE, p. 345).

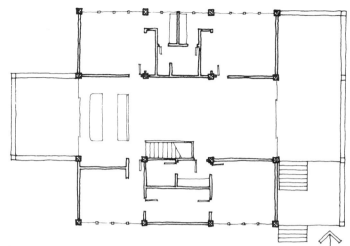

Logan House   Tampa, Florida   Rowe Holmes Assoc.

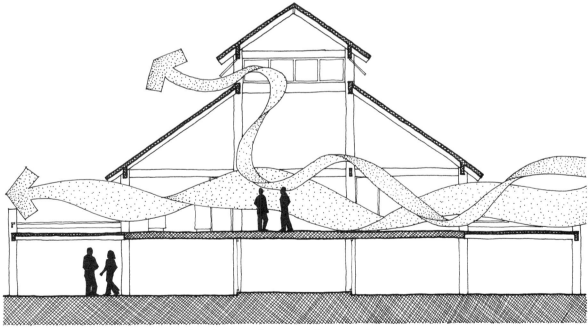

Logan House   Tampa, Florida   Rowe Holmes Assoc.

ROOMS: Zoned Organizations

44. *Rooms can be zoned within buildings to use or reject sources of internal heat gain.* *[heating and cooling]*

In many buildings, certain areas generate large quantities of heat from heavy concentrations of equipment or people. Buildings with a heating requirement can exploit these sources to supply some of the needed heat. Traditional New England houses frequently clustered their rooms around the central hearth used for cooking to share its heat. (See Rooms: Compact Organizations, Strategy 42.) These heat sources can be positioned to heat the north side, which compliments the sun-warmed south areas.

In warmer climates where cooling requirements predominate, the heat-producing elements can be isolated from the other spaces. In Robert E. Lee's home, **Stratford Hall,** in warm Virginia, the kitchen, which is a constant source of heat, is located in a separate dependency. In order to heat the main house when it is cold, fireplaces unrelated to the continuous cooking activity are used.

South Elevation Stratford Hall Virginia

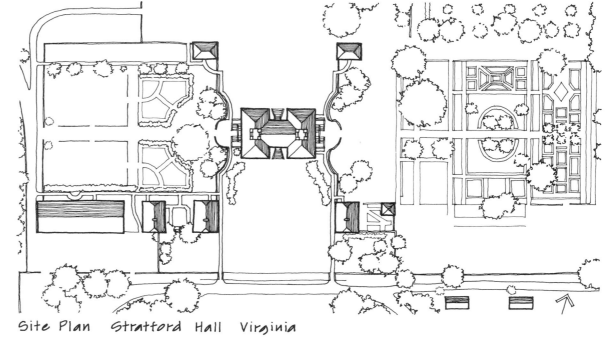

Site Plan Stratford Hall Virginia

ROOMS: Zoned Organizations

45. *Rooms can be zoned vertically within buildings to take advantage of temperature stratification. [heating]*

Because hot air rises, the upper levels of a building are frequently warmer than the lower levels. This temperature stratification can be used to zone uses or activities by temperature requirements. This phenomenon was recognized by the Inuit (Eskimo) **Igloo** builders of the Canadian north, who used the lower levels of the entrance as a cold air trap and for storage and the upper levels for living (Schoenauer, p. 28).

Ralph Erskine followed the same principle in his design for a **ski lodge at Borgafjäll** in Sweden. The circulation spaces with the least strict temperature requirements are lowest. The living/cooking quarters are on an intermediate level and the sleeping quarters, which need to be the warmest, are on the uppermost level (*Architectural Design,* 11-12/77, p. 763).

In two-story passively heated buildings that depend on natural convection as a means of heat transfer, the temperature differences between upper and lower levels have been found to be at least 4 to 5°F (Balcomb & Yamaguchi, p. 289).

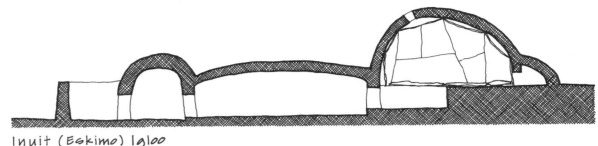

Inuit (Eskimo) Igloo

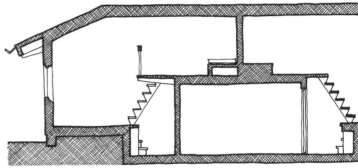

Ski Lodge Borgafjäll Ralph Erskine

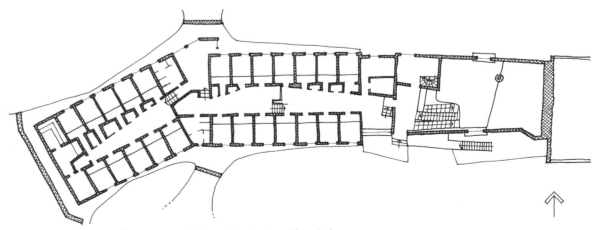

Ski Lodge Borgafjäll Ralph Erskine

46. *Rooms that can tolerate temperature swings can be used as buffer zones against heat or cold. [heating and cooling]*

Some spaces in a building's program have less rigid temperature requirements because of the nature of their use, like storage, or the duration of their use, like circulation. Some spaces, like bedrooms, have temperature requirements only at certain times of the day. These spaces can frequently be used as thermal buffer zones between spaces that need careful temperature control and the exterior environment.

Ralph Erskine used the garage and storage areas in the **Villa Gadelius** as a buffer zone against the cold north winds in Lindingö, Sweden. The south zone of the house is extended in the east–west direction and increased in height so that the living spaces have access to the south sun (*Architectural Design*, 11-12/77, p. 784).

The opposite approach was taken by Frank Lloyd Wright in the **Pauson House** in the hot Phoenix climate. The virtually unglazed circulation and storage spaces are used as a buffer zone along the west part of the house to protect the living spaces from the low, late afternoon sun (Hitchock, 1942, fig. 392).

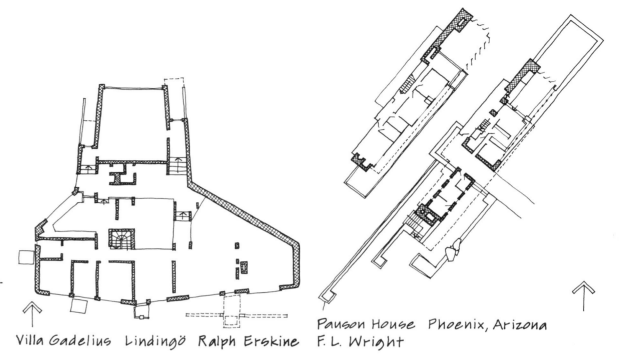

Villa Gadelius Lindingö Ralph Erskine

Pauson House Phoenix, Arizona F. L. Wright

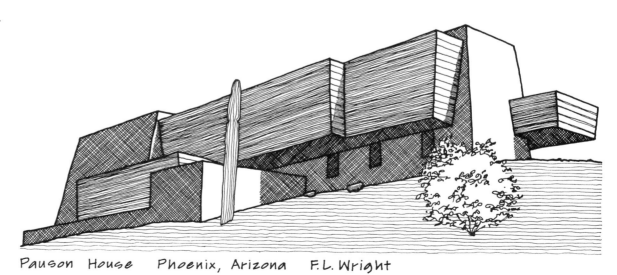

Pauson House Phoenix, Arizona F.L. Wright

ROOMS: Zoned Organizations

47. *Rooms can be zoned within the building so that activities that need higher lighting levels are near the windows and activities that don't need as much light are in darker areas.* *[daylighting]*

Many buildings have a range of activities that have varying visual tasks and therefore different illumination needs. Areas nearest the skin of the building have the greatest opportunity for daylight at the highest illumination levels. If activities are zoned so that those that need the light are placed near openings in the skin and those that don't are placed in the interior, then the amount of relatively expensive skin and glazed openings can be reduced because of a smaller skin/volume ratio.

The **Mount Angel Library** in Oregon by Alvar Aalto divides activities into two main groups: reading, which requires high levels of illumination, and book storage, which requires lower levels. The reading areas are next to openings in the skin along the perimeter wall and under the skylight in the center, while the book storage occurs between the two reading areas furthest from the pools of light.

Louis Sullivan followed a similar approach in the **Auditorium Building** in Chicago, ringing the exterior of the building with offices that need light and putting the auditorium, which needs light control, in the darker center of the building.

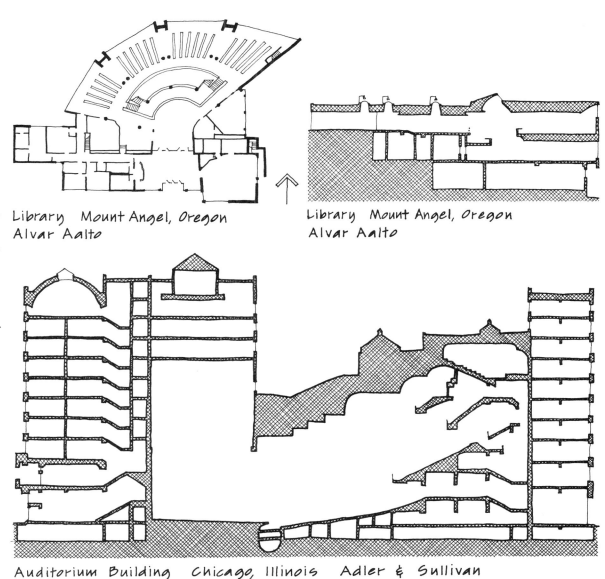

Library Mount Angel, Oregon
Alvar Aalto

Library Mount Angel, Oregon
Alvar Aalto

Auditorium Building Chicago, Illinois Adler & Sullivan

COURTYARDS: Layers

48. *An overhead layer of shades can be created to protect the courtyard from the high sun. [cooling]*

During the summer or in lower latitudes, the sun is high enough in the sky for much of the day that horizontal shading devices are more effective than vertical ones.

Because the sun changes position throughout the day, a shading device must be larger than the area to be continuously shaded. Its size must increase as the distance from the shaded area to the device increases and as the length of desired shading time increases. Obviously, as the sun moves, it will also shade adjacent areas. *From the table, the horizontal dimension of the shading device may be determined as a function of its height above the ground.* The cross-hatched area represents the continuously shaded area. Though square in the diagram, it can be any rectangular shape. The rectangle represents the shading device drawn in plan above the shaded area. The dimensions a and b are the distances, in plan, from the edge of the shaded area to the edge of the shading device.

The shading devices may be opaque or louvered as they are in this **Tucson, Arizona house** designed by Judith Chafee, where the shades partially cover the building as well as outside areas (Watson & Labs, p. 15).

The shades can be movable so that the sun can be let in when it is cold and screened when it is hot. Fixed shades have the potential disadvantage of shading equally for months on either side of June. In climates with cool springs, say March and April, it is desirable to admit the sun, but in August and September, when it is hot and sun positions are identical, shade is needed.

Unlike fixed shades, selected deciduous vines follow the climate rather than the sun's symmetry. They're in full leaf in the hottest months (August and September), but still bare and relatively transparent in March and April. The **Abramson house** in Sacramento, California, by Brent Smith, has leafy vines on its trellis to shade both the house and the deck (Wright & Andrejko, p. 90). As the Abramson house demonstrates, while the zone of shading is basically horizontal, the shading elements are not limited to horizontal planes.

House   Tucson, Arizona   Judith Chafee

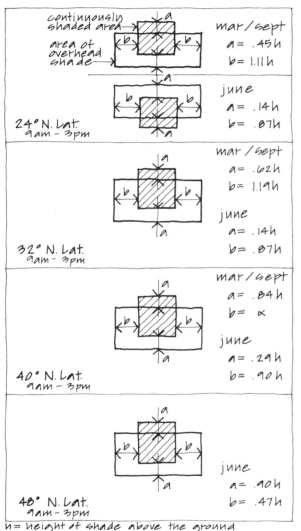

continuously shaded area
area of overhead shade

mar/sept
a = .45 h
b = 1.11 h

june
a = .14 h
b = .87 h

24° N. Lat.
9 am – 3 pm

mar/sept
a = .62 h
b = 1.19 h

june
a = .14 h
b = .87 h

32° N. Lat.
9 am – 3 pm

mar/sept
a = .84 h
b = ∝

june
a = .29 h
b = .90 h

40° N. Lat.
9 am – 3 pm

june
a = .90 h
b = .47 h

48° N. Lat.
9 am – 3 pm

h = height of shade above the ground

Size and Location of Overhead Shades

Abramson Residence   Sacramento, California   Brent Smith

COURTYARDS: Size and Shape

49. Tall and narrow courtyards can be used as cold air sinks. [cooling]

The courtyard building is a traditional and effective configuration for cooling in hot arid climates where there is a large diurnal temperature swing. *If the courtyard is higher than it is wide, it will shade some of its walls during much of the day even though the sun is high, and wind blowing over the building won't disturb the air in the court.* During the night the roof and the court, especially its floor, radiate heat to the cold night sky directly overhead. Air that is next to these surfaces cools and settles to the bottom of the court. The cold air in the court cools the surrounding surfaces, which have stored heat from the day before.

During the day the court remains comfortable because its surfaces and the ambient air are relatively cool (Koenigsberger et al., p. 205). The coolness of the court can be further enhanced by trees for shading and fountains for evaporative cooling as it is in this **house in Dubai** (Coles & Jackson, p. 22).

Alternately shaded and open courts can be used to induce air flow from one to the other. In a project by Marevil Aitchison in **Alice Springs, Australia,** courts in the center of a two-house group are heated by the sun, causing the hot air to rise and be replaced by cold air, which is then drawn through the house from the cooler shaded entrance courts (Saini, 1980, p. 90).

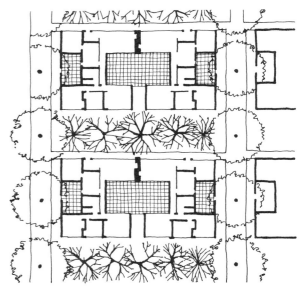

Housing Alice Springs, Australia
Marevil Aitchison

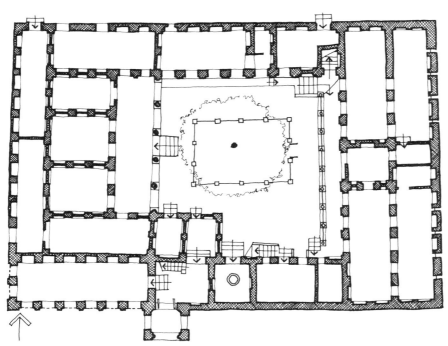

Bastakia Windtower House Dubai

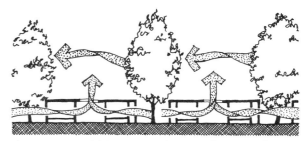

Housing Alice Springs, Australia
Marevil Aitchison

ROOMS AND COURTYARDS:
Shape and Orientation

50. *Rooms fronting or enclosing courtyards can be shaped to form sunny, wind-protected exterior spaces. [heating]*

When the temperature is below the comfort zone, the comfort of exterior spaces can be increased dramatically by admitting the sun and blocking the wind (see Technique 10). This condition occurs up to 13% of the time in cool climates like Madison, Wisconsin, and 24% of the time in warm climates like Charleston, NC (Brown & Novitski, p. 372). The usefulness of these spaces may be extended into the evening by providing masonry surfaces that will absorb the sun's heat during the day and reradiate it during the early evening. Because most U.S. climates are characterized by both underheated and overheated periods within the same day or season, the sunny, wind-protected spaces can be more useful if modified to also provide small subareas with shade and access to breeze.

When the wind blows from a direction opposite the sun position, the building can be expected to provide a sunny, wind-protected area as long as three to four times the building height (Melaragno, pp. 347, 377). When the wind and the sun both come from the same direction, a shelter belt or windscreen may be used on the south side of the court because the wind shadow is several times longer than the sun's shadow at most times of the day and in most seasons (Melaragno, p. 380). At **Tigbourne Court** in Surrey, England, by Edwin Lutyens, the distribution of major rooms is quite different than one would expect from the symmetrical west facade. The east–west entrance axis is blocked by a stairway and the circulation turns 90° to the major rooms, which are distributed along a south-facing terrace.

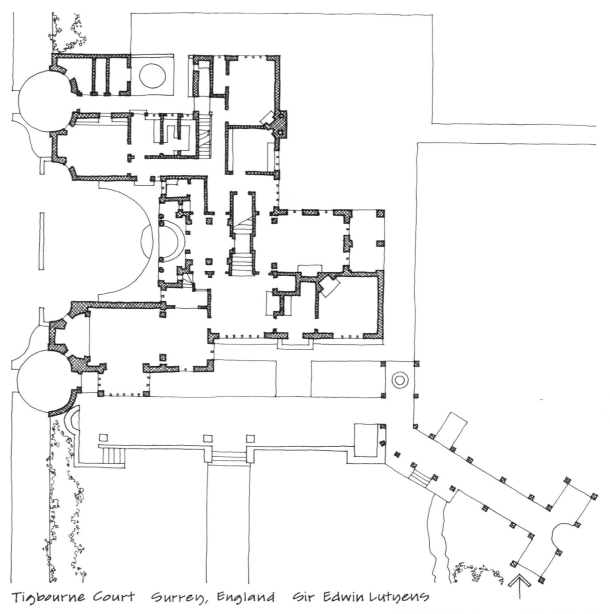

Tigbourne Court   Surrey, England   Sir Edwin Lutyens

ROOMS AND COURTYARDS:
Zoned Organizations

51. *Rooms and courts can be zoned so that activities can take place in cooler areas during warm periods and warmer areas during cool periods of the day or season [heating and cooling]*

This strategy combines migration—moving from one place to another to maintain thermal comfort—with providing a variety of zones, each of which is comfortable under a different set of climatic conditions. Because each zone is tuned to a limited set of conditions, its design can be simpler. Design criteria can be selected that do no more than simply moderate climatic extremes; they may take advantage of the beneficial relationship between some materials' thermal characteristics and certain climate patterns, such as thermal lag and large diurnal temperature swings; or they may exploit the compatability of certain climate conditions with existing social patterns, like moving from a living to a sleeping area.

Pueblo Acoma is an example of a two-zone residence in which the time of day that each zone is used changes dramatically from season to season.

In cool seasons, the outside terraces are used during the day and the interior spaces at night. In the warm seasons the reverse is true: the outside terraces are used at night and the shaded cool interiors during the day.

One zone, the exterior south-facing terrace, is wind-protected and sunny during the day, an advantage when the air is cool and a disadvantage when it is warm. It radiates heat to the sky at night, an advantage when it's warm and a disadvantage when it's cool. The second zone, the interior room, follows the outside climate less closely than the terrace. The

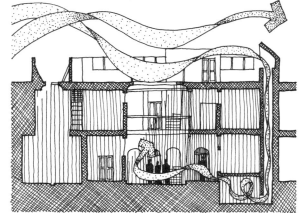

Iraq House   Summer Day

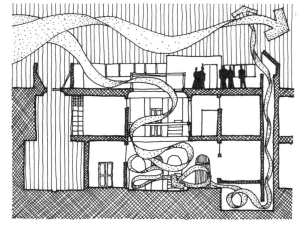

Iraq House   Summer Night

Pueblo Acoma   Warm Season Day

Warm Season Night

Pueblo Acoma   Cool Season Day

Cool Season Night

heat storage characteristics of the massive construction cause the interior temperature to lag several hours behind the exterior temperature. In the cool seasons the mass absorbs the sun's heat during the day and releases it to the interior at night. In warm seasons, the mass is cooled at night by the air and by radiation to the sky, and so remains cool during the day.

This **house in Iraq** is zoned vertically; the use of these layers changes both daily and seasonally. The court and chimneys, combined with the building's massive construction, effectively moderate the high summer temperatures. During the summer day, people live on the first level, which is cooled by several strategies. The incoming breezes are directed into the wind catchers at the top of the chimneys; the air is cooled by the mass of the chimneys and falls to rooms or to the basement, where it is further cooled by evaporation before it flows into the court. The court, which is tall enough to be partially protected from the sun, is sprinkled daily to cool its air. On summer evenings, people sleep on the roof, which is cooled by radiation to the night sky. At night, the cool air from the roof falls into the court, flows through the building, cooling the mass heated during the day, and exits up the warm chimney.

During the short mild winter, the family lives on the second level, away from the cool court floor. In the transitional periods of spring and fall when the roof is too cool and the rooms are too warm, the second level gallery is used for sleeping (Al-Azzawi, p. 91).

Thermal zones were designed for this **residence in Grants Pass, Oregon,** by Equinox Design, Inc., to organize activities and passive heating and cooling systems. The zones are graded from most thermally controlled to least. The building expands and contracts daily and seasonally with movable walls so that

its heating and cooling loads remain fairly constant even when outdoor temperatures vary. System characteristics are matched with zone characteristics. For example, trombe walls, which supply even heat, are located in the most thermally stable enclaves.

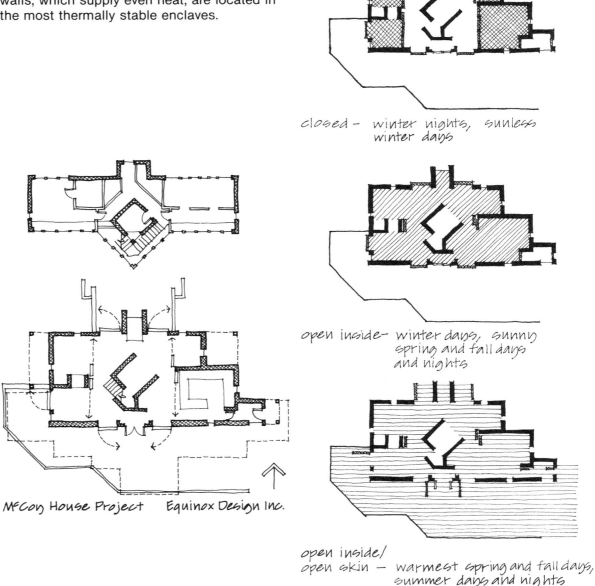

closed — winter nights, sunless winter days

open inside — winter days, sunny spring and fall days and nights

open inside/ open skin — warmest spring and fall days, summer days and nights

McCoy House Project   Equinox Design Inc.

C

Building Parts

Design strategies at this scale deal with the parts used to make rooms, courtyards, and buildings. They are the skin elements—walls, roofs, and floors—and openings in the skin, windows.

Several of the strategies (Strategies 52, 55, 59, and 60) deal with size of those parts, ranging from wall thickness to window area. Three strategies (53, 54, 58) address color, one concerned with dark colors that absorb radiation and two with light colors that reflect light, thus reducing contrast and evening the distribution of light. Two strategies (56 and 57) discuss the placement of insulation and its impact on the design of walls and windows. The remaining strategies (65 and 68) address the frequently combined issues of shading and daylighting.

WALLS, ROOFS, AND FLOORS: Size

52. *The building's skin should be thick enough to accommodate the required insulation. [heating and cooling]*

There are two basic strategies for locating thermal insulation. In one, the insulation is contained within the skin cavity; in the other, the insulation is applied to the surface of the skin. At low, thin insulation levels, when insulation is placed within the hollow skin between the framing members, the overall thickness of the wall can be less than with solid walls which must have the insulation on their surface.

When the insulation is placed on the surface of the skin, such as on the inside surface of an exterior brick wall, one side of the skin material can be left exposed, and the framing members do not need to be increased in size to accommodate thicker layers of insulation. The two strategies can be combined, with some insulation placed on the skin's surface and some between the framing members.

Recommended insulation levels for skin-dominated solar-heated buildings are based on balancing the cost/benefit of conservation (reducing loss) with passive solar strategies (increasing gain) (Balcomb, 1983, p. 117).

Recommended insulation levels for skin-dominated passively cooled buildings are based on maintaining a temperature difference between inside and out and on reducing solar gain. If cooling strategies like cross-ventilation and stack-ventilation are used, the inside temperature is slightly higher than the outside, so insulation isn't needed to reduce the heat flow due to the temperature difference. It is needed only to reduce the heat flow due to solar radiation. If walls and roofs are protected from solar gain, insulation levels can be significantly reduced.

Insulation thickness in inches can be approximated by dividing the recommended insulation levels from the maps by 3 for fiberglass batt insulation and by 4 to 6 for rigid insulation.

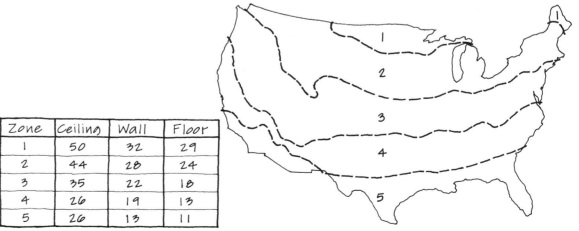

Zone	Ceiling	Wall	Floor
1	50	32	29
2	44	28	24
3	35	22	18
4	26	19	13
5	26	13	11

Recommended Minimum Thermal Resistances (R) of Insulation

WALLS, ROOFS, AND FLOORS: Color

53. *Massive thermal storage surfaces should be dark in color to absorb radiation, and nonmassive surfaces should be light in color to reflect radiation. [heating]*

Materials used to absorb and store solar radiation should be at least 50% absorbent to optimize the amount of solar radiation they absorb (Balcomb, Barley, et al., p. 74). If a mass surface is the first to be struck by the sun but is a small part of the total mass area, then that surface should be moderately reflective so that radiation is spread to other absorbing surfaces. The surfaces of light-weight, non-massive materials should be light in color so that they will reflect light to the massive surfaces and not overheat and raise the room air temperature (Balcomb, Jones, et al., p. 57).

optical flat black paint	0.98
flat black paint	0.95
black lacquer	0.92
dark gray paint	0.91
black concrete	0.91
dark blue lacquer	0.91
black oil paint	0.90
stafford blue bricks	0.89
dark olive drab paint	0.89
dark brown paint	0.88
dark blue-gray paint	0.88
azure blue or dark green lacquer	0.88
brown concrete	0.85
medium brown paint	0.84
medium light brown paint	0.80
brown or green lacquer	0.79
medium rust paint	0.78
light gray oil paint	0.75
red oil paint	0.74
red bricks	0.70
uncolored concrete	0.65
moderately light buff bricks	0.60
medium dull green paint	0.59
medium orange paint	0.58
medium yellow paint	0.57
medium blue paint	0.51
medium kelly green paint	0.51
light green paint	0.47
white semi-gloss paint	0.30
white gloss paint	0.25
silver paint	0.25
white lacquer	0.21
polished aluminum reflector sheet	0.12
aluminized mylar film	0.10
laboratory vapor deposited coatings	0.02

Solar Absorptance of Various Materials

WALLS, ROOFS, AND FLOORS: Color

54. *Light-colored surfaces reflect daylight and increase the lighting level in the space.* [daylighting]

As one moves away from a daylight source, whether window or skylight, the amount of light provided directly from the sky decreases, and the proportion provided by reflection from interior surfaces increases. For example, in a sidelit room, with the depth approximately equal to twice the height and the glazing area equal to about 20% of the floor area, the illumination 10 feet from the window is 62% from the sky and 38% from internal reflections. Twenty feet from the window, 44% of the illumination is from the sky and 66% from reflections (Hopkinson et al., p. 442). The reflectivity of the interior surfaces is extremely important in enhancing the internally reflected component of the daylight factor, which is a substantial part of the illumination level away from the window. For example, the internally reflected light in our sidelit room changes from a daylight factor of 0.1% to 1.1% to 3.4% as the reflectance of interior surfaces varies from 10% to 40% to 80% (Hopkinson et al., p. 441).

It is important that the surface that first reflects the light be light in color to increase the amount of light reflected into the space. This surface may be the floor when light is coming directly from the sky, or the ceiling if the light is being reflected from exterior ground surfaces.

In the main auditorium at the **Institute of Technology, at Otaniemi,** Aalto used light-colored baffles and upper ceiling surfaces to completely spread the south sunlight around the auditorium space (Fleig, p. 88).

white	80-90%
pale yellow, rose	80%
pale beige, lilac	70%
pale blue, green	70-75%
mustard yellow	35%
medium brown	25%
medium blue, green	20-30%
black	10%

Reflectance of Colors

ceilings	70-80%
walls	40-80%
floors	20-40%

Recommended Reflectances

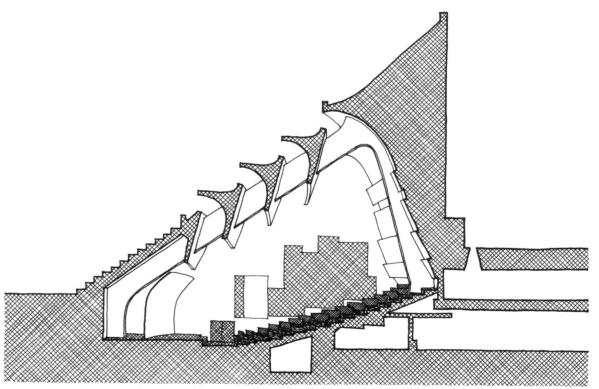

Main Auditorium Institute of Technology, Otaniemi   Alvar Aalto

WALLS AND FLOORS:
Size and Materials

55. *Thermal mass surfaces should be large enough and thick enough to store adequate heat and cold. [heating and cooling]*

There are two basic approaches one may take in sizing the area and thickness of thermal mass. The first is appropriate for storage systems like trombe walls, roof ponds, and sunspaces where the collection area defines the surface area of the mass storage and mass thickness is the primary consideration.

The second is more appropriate for direct gain and night ventilation of mass systems, where both mass surface area and thickness are variable. Because the storage mass is in the inhabited space in both direct gain and night ventilation schemes, air and mass temperatures can't be allowed to get too high or too low, so these systems depend on the large transfer areas afforded by relatively thin masonry masses. When water is used for storage, the surface areas can be smaller because heat is transferred more readily between the surface and the bulk of the mass in water than it is in masonry.

In direct gain systems, assuming the mass is in the same zone as the south aperture, so that mass surfaces can exchange long-wave radiation and reflect short-wave radiation, the masonry mass thickness should be 4 inches or more, and the surface area should be 3 to 6 sq. ft. of mass per square foot of south-facing glazing. If water is the storage medium, use 3.5 to 6.5 gal. per sq. ft. of south-facing glazing (Balcomb, Barley, et al., p. 26). The greater the amount of mass area within this range the better the performance, especially in buildings in which a large percentage of the heat is supplied by solar energy.

In night ventilation of mass schemes, the cooling benefit increases indefinitely as a function of mass area, so there is no optimum area based solely on cooling concerns. The mass area tends to be limited by the architectural surface area available, to approximately 1.5 to 3.0 sq. ft. of mass per square foot of floor.

By definition, the mass surface area of trombe walls, roof ponds, and sunspaces with storage walls between the sunspace and the room is equal to the area of the glazing. The thickness of the walls and roofs determines the amount of heat they can store and when the heat will be released. Masonry trombe walls and water walls should be 9 to 12″ thick (Balcomb, Barley, et al., p. 90). Buildings that receive a large percentage of their heating from the sun should use the thickest walls within that range.

Sunspaces are assumed to have a masonry wall between the sunspace and the room; this should be 9 to 12″ thick (Balcomb, Jones, et al., p. 95). Sunspaces with an insulated wall between the sunspace and the room that heat the room by convection should have 0.5 to 1.0 cubic feet (3.5 to 7.5 gal.) or more of water per square foot of south-facing glazing within the sunspace.

Roof ponds used for cooling usually cover the entire roof area of a single story building and therefore have a one-to-one ratio of mass area to floor area. Pond depths are usually 6 to 10 inches (Fleischnacker et al., p. 835; Mazria, p. 187).

	mass type	surface area of mass in sq. ft. per sq. ft. of floor area	surface area of mass in sq. ft. per sq. ft. of south facing glazing	thickness of mass	volume of mass in c.ft. and gal. per sq. ft. of south facing glazing
heating					
direct gain	masonry	—	3 – 6	4″ +	—
	water	—	3	—	.5 to .9 c.f. 3.5 to 6.5 gal.
trombe	masonry	—	1	9 – 12″	—
	water	—	1	9 – 12″	—
sunspace	masonry	—	1	9 – 12″	—
	water	—	*	—	.5 to 1.0 c.f. 3.5 to 7.5 gal.
cooling					
roof pond	water	1	—	6 – 10″	—
night ventilation of mass	masonry	1.5 to 3	—	2″ +	—

* water containers are assumed to line the east-west wall of the sunspace

Thermal Mass Thickness and Area

WALLS: Materials and Location

56. *Thermal insulation placed on the outside of massive thermal storage walls allows the mass to absorb heat and cold and stabilize the room air temperature. [heating and cooling]*

Masonry materials are usually regarded as exterior finish materials. However, in order to be effective thermal masses for storing heat or cold, they must have exposed surfaces inside the space. Therefore, the insulation must be between the mass and the outside air. In order to achieve a masonry exterior finish, an additional layer of masonry must be added. In the **Stockebrand House,** in Albuquerque, New Mexico, by Edward Mazria & Associates, urethane insulation was sprayed on the outside of filled concrete block. It was then covered with stucco colored to match the surrounding ground and detailed to recall the New Mexico adobe traditions (*Progressive Architecture,* 4/81).

In the **Roberts residence** in Reston, Virginia, a masonry inner house is surrounded by a highly insulated wood frame wrapper (Wright & Andrejko, p. 115).

Batt and fill insulations have an R-value of 3 to 4 per inch; rigid insulation, 4 to 6 per inch. (See Walls, Roofs, and Floors: Size, Strategy 52 for recommended insulation levels.)

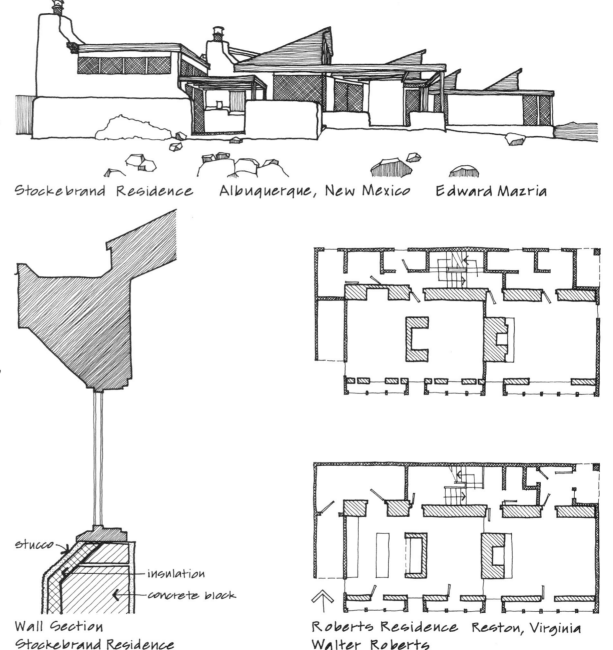

Stockebrand Residence   Albuquerque, New Mexico   Edward Mazria

stucco

insulation

concrete block

Wall Section
Stockebrand Residence

Roberts Residence Reston, Virginia
Walter Roberts

ROOFS: Shape and Material

57. *Roofs can be used as reflecting surfaces to increase the solar radiation entering south-facing glazing. [heating]*

Reflective exterior surfaces can augment the amount of radiation entering south-facing openings. The amount of radiation reflected into the opening depends on the angle between the reflector and the opening, the size and reflectivity of the reflector, and the latitude of the building site.

Any reflective surface, including the ground, with the correct relationship to the south-facing opening can be used. *For vertical openings, the reflector length should be one to two times the height of the opening, and the reflector width should be approximately the same as the opening width. The angle between them should be 90° ± 5°, depending on latitude.* A reflector with 80% reflectance sized this way will enhance the radiation entering a vertical south-facing window by 30 to 40% (Mazria, p. 241).

The **Lane Energy Center** in Cottage Grove, Oregon, by Equinox Design, Inc., uses an aluminized roofing material to reflect winter sunlight into the building clerestory. The sunlight is reflected from the building's ceiling down to the concrete floor and the water barrels on the rear wall for heat storage.

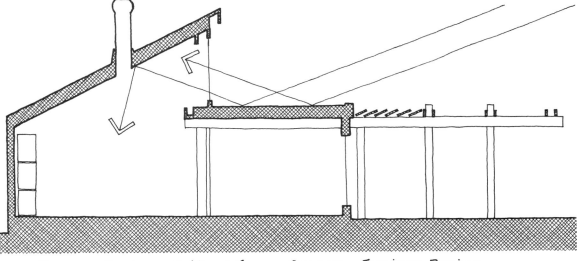

Lane Energy Center   Cottage Grove, Oregon   Equinox Design

WALLS AND WINDOWS:
Shape and Color

58. *Reducing contrast between the window frame and the adjacent walls will reduce glare and improve vision. [daylighting]*

One cause of glare is a sharp contrast between the window and its surround (Hopkinson et al., p. 330). The contrast can be reduced by minimizing the size of mullions within the window, splaying them and the adjacent wall so that they are illuminated by the window, and painting them a light color.

If the walls are thick, as they are in **Thomas Jefferson's rotunda** at the University of Virginia (B. Evans, p. 72), it is relatively easy to achieve the light gradations between the wall and the window. If the wall is thin, additional reflecting surfaces at the edge of the window may be achieved by projecting the window out from the wall.

The area of gradation around the window in the window wall is valuable up to a distance of 10 times the window dimensions. Effective reveals are 9 to 12" deep, at an angle of 60° to the plane of the window, and 60 to 90% reflective. The window wall itself should be a light color.

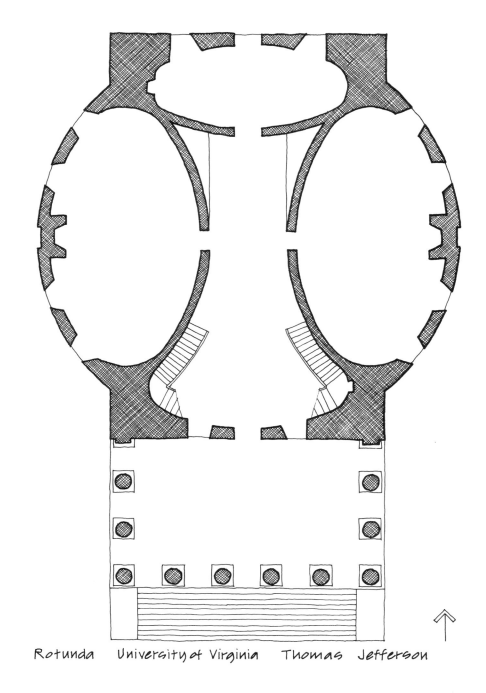

Rotunda   University of Virginia   Thomas Jefferson

WINDOWS: Size

59. *Increasing the window size will increase interior illumination levels. [daylighting]*

The amount of light that reaches the interior of a room is a function of wall and ceiling reflectance, window placement and size, room proportion and size, and external obstructions. For a room with average proportions, surface reflectances of approximately 40%, and no external obstructions, the average amount of light in the space is directly proportional to the area of the glazing (Hopkinson et al., p. 432). Locations within the room will vary considerably from the average as a function of their proximity to the windows. For windows that are large relative to the wall area, the average reflected value of the interior surfaces falls below 40%, and the glazing area becomes a less accurate indicator of average illumination.

The graphs may be used to determine the glazing area needed to achieve a certain average daylight factor for a given floor area or to determine the average daylight factor for given floor and glazing areas under overcast sky conditions. The sidelighting daylight factors apply to a zone with a depth into the room of three times the height of the window wall. If more than one opening type is used for the same area, the daylight factors may be added. An example of using more than one opening type is Albert Kahn's use of sidelighting and monitors in the **Packard Forge Shop** in Detroit (Hildebrand, p. 57).

Recommended daylight factors are shown in the table (Hopkinson, p. 22).

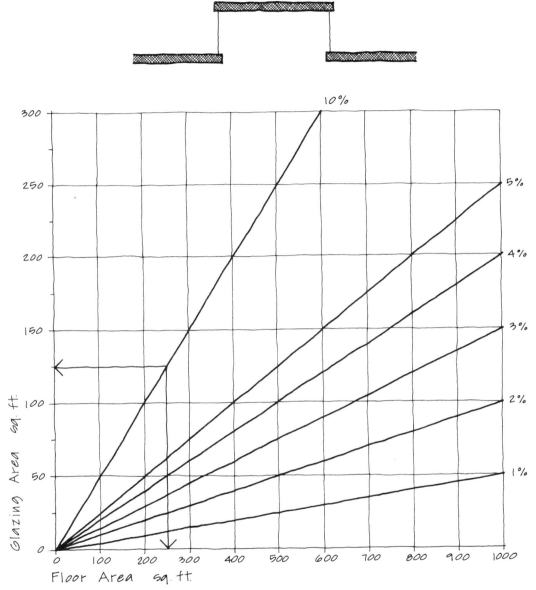

Daylight Factors for Sidelighting and Vertical Monitors

Building Type	Recommended Daylight Factor %
Dwellings	
Kitchen	2
Living room	1
Bedroom	0.5
Schools	2
Hospitals	1
Offices	
General	1 to 2
	2
Drawing offices	2
(on drawing boards)	6
Typing and computing	4
Laboratories	3 to 6
Factories	5
Art galleries	6
Churches	1 to 2
Public buildings	1

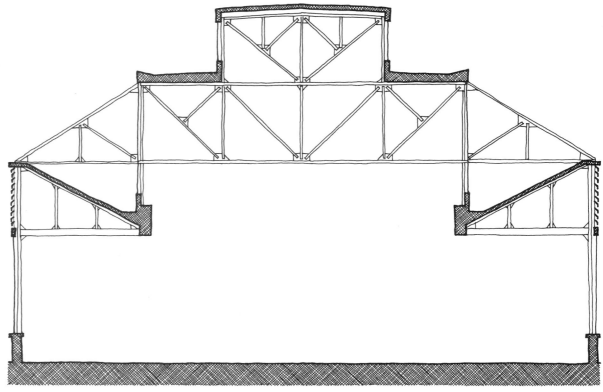

Packard Forge Shop   Detroit, Michigan   Albert Kahn

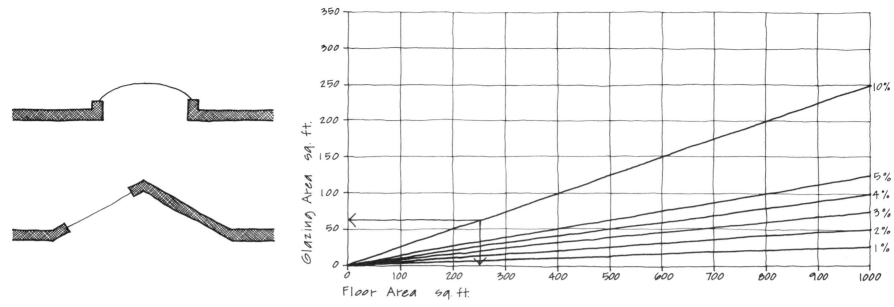

Daylight Factors for Horizontal and 30° Sloped Glazing

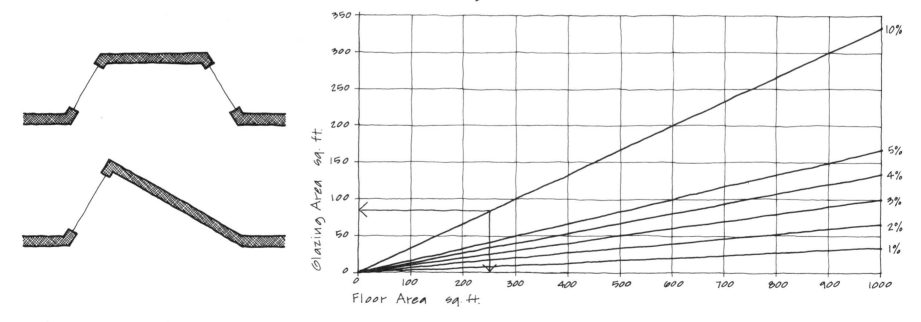

Daylight Factors for 60° Sloped Roof and Monitor Glazing

WINDOWS: Size

60. *Openings that collect solar radiation can be enlarged to increase the percentage of the annual heating requirement supplied by solar energy. [heating]*

The percentage of the annual heating load that can be supplied by the sun is determined by a delicate balance between the amount of solar radiation that can be collected, the amount of heat loss, and the amount of heat that can be stored during the day for use at night. Collectible radiation is a function of the amount of south-facing glazing and the radiation available in the climate. Heat loss is a function of the insulating qualities of the building skin and the severity of the climate. The amount of solar radiation collected that is usable for heating the interior is a function of the system's operating characteristics.

The **Brookhaven House,** a prototype designed by Total Environmental Action, uses three systems—direct gain, sunspace and trombe walls —to meet its heating requirements. (See Strategies 33, 34, and 35 for a more complete explanation of these systems.)

The trombe wall, which is punctured by a direct gain window, is located at the end of the dining room; the sunspace, which is separated from the kitchen and family room by a mass storage wall, completes the south side of the lower floor. Direct gain windows are used on the second floor bedrooms. The second floor also has a balcony that opens to the sunspace. The house is designed so that the entry can be located either in the sunspace or the porch, so the house can be built with either side facing the street and still have the solar-collecting surfaces facing south. It is estimated that the sun will supply this house with 65% of its heating requirements in Bos·

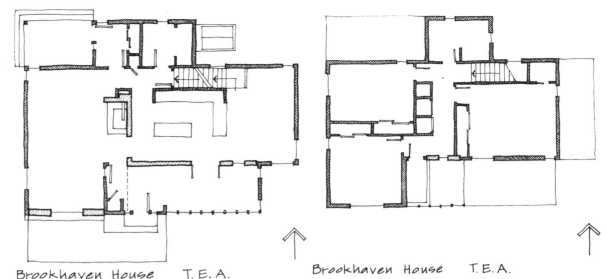

Brookhaven House   T.E.A.   Brookhaven House   T.E.A.

Brookhaven House   Total Environmental Action, Inc.

ton, 65% in New York, 57% in Chicago, 77% in Baltimore, 56% in Madison, Wisconsin, and 69% in Louisville, Kentucky (*Solar Age,* 1/80, p. 56).

The solar savings fraction is the percentage of energy saved by using solar energy to heat a building compared to a nonsolar building with similar thermal characteristics (Balcomb, Jones, et al., p. 5). *The chart estimates the solar savings fraction for six United States locations as a function of the percentage of floor area in south-facing glazing.*

The data, while specific to each location, represent a wide range of conditions in the United States, based on the heating degree days and the daily average radiation incident on a vertical surface in January (Balcomb, Jones, et al., p. 47). Albuquerque is cool and very sunny, Boston is cold and cloudy, Madison is very cold and cloudy, Medford is cool and very cloudy, Nashville is cool and cloudy, and Santa Maria is mild and sunny.

Select the city that most closely matches the characteristics of your site. Degree days may be found in Balcomb, Jones, et al., p. 260; Packard, p. 45; and Mazria, p. 404. Radiation may be found in Balcomb, Jones, et al., p. 260; Mazria, pp. 366 and 384; and Kusuda and Ishii.

The following assumptions were made about heat loss in each location: Albuquerque, Medford, and Nashville—5.6 Btu per DD per sq. ft.; Boston—4.6 Btu per DD per sq. ft.; Madison—3.6 Btu per DD per sq. ft.; and Santa Maria—6.6 Btu per DD per sq ft.

The direct gain system is assumed to be double glazed with 6 sq. ft. of 4-" thick masonry mass for each square foot of south-facing glazing.

The sunspace is assumed to be attached, with a common 12-" thick masonry wall, 50° sloped glazing, opaque insulated east and

Percentage of Floor Area in South Facing Glazing	Albuquerque NM	Boston MA	Madison WI	Medford OR	Nashville TN	SantaMaria CA	
10	30-40	10-20	–	20-30	10-20	50-60	no night insulation
10	40-50	20-30	20-30	30-40	30-40	60-70	with R-9 night insulation
20	60-70	10-20	–	30-40	20-30	80-90	
20	70-80	40-50	40-50	50-60	50-60	80-90	
30	70-80	–	–	30-40	30-40	80-90	
30	80-90	60-70	60-70	60-70	60-70	+	
40	70-80	–	–	30-40	40-50	+	
40	+	60-70	60-70	60-70	70-80	+	
50	–	–	–	–	40-50	+	
50	+	70-80	70-80	70-80	80-90	+	
60	–	–	–	–	40-50	+	
60	+	70-80	70-80	80-90	80-90	+	
70	–	–	–	–	–	+	
70	+	80-90	70-80	80-90	80-90	+	
80	–	–	–	–	–	+	
80	+	80-90	70-80	80-90	+	+	
90	–	–	–	–	–	+	
90	+	80-90	70-80	80-90	+	+	

– solar savings fraction greater than previously listed cannot be achieved
+ maximum solar savings fraction can be achieved with less % glazing

Solar Savings Fraction (%) – Direct Gain

west walls, and double glazing. The data given approximate the performance of other similar sunspace configurations.

The trombe wall system is a vented, 12-" thick masonry wall that is double glazed.

Substantial variations in the amount or type of mass, the area of venting, or the number of glazings will alter the solar savings fractions of these systems. An extensive list of systems and their performance may be found in Balcomb, Jones, et al., p. 344.

Percentage of Floor Area in South Facing Glazing	Albuquerque NM	Boston MA	Madison WI	Medford OR	Nashville TN	Santa Maria CA	
10	40-50	20-30	20-30	20-30	20-30	60-70	no night insulation
	50-60	30-40	30-40	30-40	30-40	70-80	with R-9 night insulation
20	60-70	30-40	30-40	30-40	40-50	80-90	
	70-80	40-50	40-50	50-60	50-60	80-90	
30	70-80	40-50	30-40	40-50	40-50	80-90	
	80-90	50-60	50-60	60-70	60-70	+	
40	80-90	40-50	30-40	50-60	50-60	+	
	+	60-70	60-70	60-70	70-80	+	
50	80-90	50-60	40-50	50-60	60-70	+	
	+	70-80	70-80	70-80	80-90	+	
60	+	50-60	40-50	50-60	60-70	+	
	+	70-80	70-80	70-80	80-90	+	
70	+	50-60	40-50	60-70	70-80	+	
	+	70-80	70-80	70-80	80-90	+	
80	+	50-60	40-50	60-70	70-80	+	
	+	80-90	70-80	80-90	+	+	
90	+	60-70	40-50	60-70	70-80	+	
	+	80-90	80-90	80-90	+	+	

+ maximum solar savings fraction can be achieved with less % glazing

Solar Savings Fraction (%) — Sun Space

Percentage of Floor Area in South Facing Glazing	Albuquerque NM	Boston MA	Madison WI	Medford OR	Nashville TN	Santa Maria CA	
10	30 – 40	10 – 20	10 – 20	20 – 30	20 – 30	50 – 60	no night insulation
	40 – 50	20 – 30	20 – 30	30 – 40	30 – 40	60 – 70	with R-9 night insulation
20	50 – 60	20 – 30	20 – 30	30 – 40	30 – 40	70 – 80	
	70 – 80	40 – 50	40 – 50	40 – 50	50 – 60	80 – 90	
30	70 – 80	30 – 40	30 – 40	40 – 50	40 – 50	80 – 90	
	80 – 90	50 – 60	50 – 60	50 – 60	60 – 70	+	
40	80 – 90	30 – 40	30 – 40	40 – 50	50 – 60	+	
	+	60 – 70	60 – 70	60 – 70	70 – 80	+	
50	80 – 90	40 – 50	30 – 40	50 – 60	50 – 60	+	
	+	70 – 80	70 – 80	70 – 80	70 – 80	+	
60	+	40 – 50	40 – 50	50 – 60	60 – 70	+	
	+	70 – 80	70 – 80	70 – 80	80 – 90	+	
70	+	50 – 60	40 – 50	50 – 60	60 – 70	+	
	+	80 – 90	80 – 90	80 – 90	80 – 90	+	
80	+	50 – 60	40 – 50	60 – 70	70 – 80	+	
	+	80 – 90	80 – 90	80 – 90	80 – 90	+	
90	+	50 – 60	40 – 50	60 – 70	70 – 80	+	
	+	80 – 90	80 – 90	80 – 90	+	+	

+ maximum solar savings fraction can be achieved with less % glazing

Solar Savings Fraction (%) – Trombe Wall

WINDOWS: Size and Orientation

61. *Heat loss can be reduced by limiting the area of nonsouth windows. [heating]*

Within well-insulated skin-dominated load buildings, the primary causes of heat loss are infiltration and windows. The size, number, and orientation of windows greatly affect the building's energy use for heating. In the daytime during the heating season, windows are simultaneously losing heat because it's warmer inside than out and gaining heat because direct or diffuse solar radiation is passing through the glass and heating the interior. At night, of course, the windows only lose heat. If a window gains more heat than it loses over the course of the heating season, it reduces the heating requirements of the building. Windows that don't face south usually lose more energy than they gain and therefore increase the building's heating requirements. The amenities of non–south-facing windows, such as view, light, and ventilation, should be carefully weighed against their thermal liability in the heating season.

In the **Glessner House,** H.H. Richardson concentrated the major living spaces and most of the glazing on the south side of the building, overlooking a sun-filled court. The service spaces and circulation, which require little glazing, are located along the north edge of the building (Hitchcock, 1936, p. 128). This maximizes the window area that gains heat from the sun and minimizes that which does not.

Assuming a well-insulated solar-heated building (Balcomb, Barley, et al., p. 24) and an infiltration rate of .75 air changes per hour, *the nonsouth double glazed windows should be limited to 5 to 10% of the non-south-facing wall area.*

J.J. Glessner House   Chicago, Illinois   H.H. Richardson

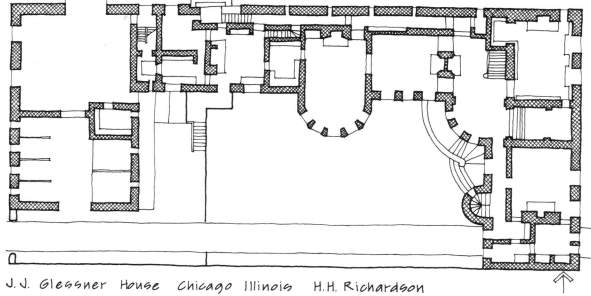

J.J. Glessner House   Chicago Illinois   H.H. Richardson

WINDOWS: Size and Orientation

62. *Reflected sunlight can be used for daylighting in clear-sky climates. [daylighting]*

Buildings that use daylighting to reduce their level of electric lighting and thus their cooling requirements are common in clear-sky climates. The dominant source of illumination in a clear sky is the sun and the area immediately around it. (See Climate as a Context, Technique 8.) Because the sun is an extremely powerful light source, providing up to 10,000 footcandles, but also a source of heat gain of up to 300 Btu per hr. per sq. ft., it is important to balance the lighting benefits against heat gain detriments. The illumination levels inside a building are up to 1,000 times less than they are outside, so a small amount of sunlight can be distributed over a large area and still provide adequate illumination. The goal is to meet minimum illumination levels through as much of the day as possible without exceeding the minimum because excess light also means excess heat gain.

There are two basic strategies for using the sun for lighting while minimizing heat gain. The first is to use a very small window opening (at most, 10 to 20% of the wall area) to illuminate a surface inside the space that then spreads the light out over a large area. The second is to use a moderately sized window that "sees" an exterior reflective surface but is shaded from the direct sun.

In the hot sunny Dallas, Texas, climate, Louis Kahn used small openings in the top of the vaults of the **Kimbell Museum** to let in sunlight. The light was reflected from an internal reflector onto the ceiling, which in turn reflected it onto the walls and floor (B. Evans, p. 158).

Kahn made use of exterior reflecting surfaces in the **Chancellery building** for Luanda, Angola, by creating a court outside each office so that the windows receive only sunlight reflected from the court walls and ground (Scully, p. 35).

The amount of illumination available to a window from the sun changes dramatically with the sun position, but the exterior illumination available from direct sunlight, ground reflectance, and light reflected from vertical walls remains relatively constant throughout the day with the exception of the hours just after sunrise and before sunset. As a consequence, shaded windows that face courts or streets with buildings on the other side have a relatively constant source of illumination.

Building users can be protected from glare by locating the openings out of their direct line of sight if the windows are admitting direct sunlight or by reducing the luminance of the reflecting surfaces visible from the window.

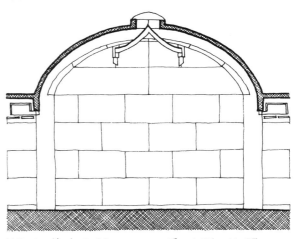

Kimbell Art Museum Fort Worth, Texas
Louis I. Kahn

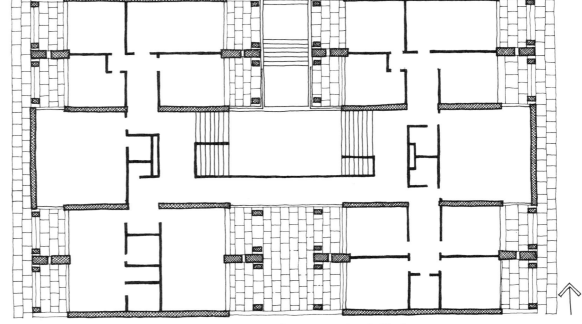

Chancellery U.S. Consulate Luanda Louis I. Kahn

WINDOWS: Location and Orientation

63. *Openings for ventilation, light, and solar gain may be separated or combined. [heating, cooling, daylighting]*

When building components such as windows are designed to perform a single function, like ventilation, solar gain, or lighting, their design may be very specific to that function, and they have a better chance of performing it well. Combining various functions in a single component allows the cost of the component to be justified in terms of several attributes. Depending on the climate and building type, the functions of ventilating, solar gain, and lighting may be strongly related over the entire year, may be related for some time periods but unrelated for others, or may be completely unrelated for the entire year.

The roof monitors in this **office building in Fairfax, Virginia,** combine the tasks of solar heating, daylighting, and ventilating. The 10′ × 10′ monitors occur in each 30′ × 30′ bay of this largely underground building. The monitors change their role seasonally: they provide solar heating in the winter and daylighting and stack ventilating in the summer (*Progressive Architecture,* 4/82, p. 138).

In the **Social Security Administration, Northeast Program Service Center** by the Gruzen partnership, The Ehrenkrantz Group, and Syska & Hennessy, windows for daylighting and windows for view are treated as separate components. The windows for daylighting form a continuous strip high in the wall. The windows for view are spaced periodically below the daylighting strip. They are all glazed as one unit of which the top is primarily for light and the bottom is for view (Vonier, p. 155).

In the **Pension Building** in Washington, D.C., which has a ring of offices around a cen-

One University Plaza   Fairfax, Virginia   Alternative Design

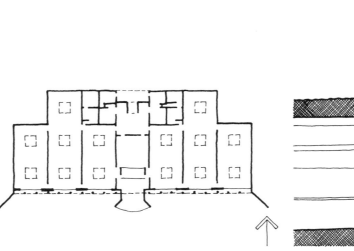

One University Plaza   Fairfax, Virginia
Alternative Design

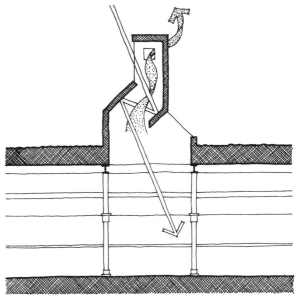

One University Plaza   Fairfax, Virginia
Alternative Design

tral atrium, architect Montgomery C. Meigs separated the functions of fresh air ventilation and daylighting by putting vents below each window. Air can flow through the offices, be warmed, rise, and finally be exhausted through the clerestories in the atrium (Smith, p. 63).

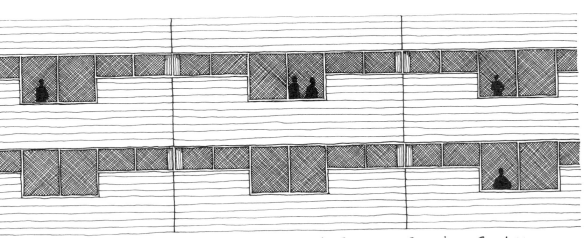

Social Security Administration, Northeast Program Service Center
Gruzen Partnership, The Ehrenkrantz Group and Syska & Hennessy

Social Security Administration, Northeast Program Service Center
Gruzen Partnership, The Ehrenkrantz Group and Syska & Hennessy

Pension Building Washington, D.C.
Montgomery C. Meigs

WINDOWS: Location and Orientation

64. *Ventilation openings can be arranged to move air across occupants to increase their rate of cooling. [cooling]*

In addition to removing hot air from a space, ventilation can also affect cooling, if the air is moving fast enough, by increasing the rate of evaporation from the skin of the occupants. When the outside ambient air temperature is above the comfort zone, vents should be designed for occupant cooling as well as for heat removal. Use the bioclimatic chart from Technique 10 in Climate as a Context to determine the wind speed that will create comfort for given air temperatures. The average interior air velocity is a function of the exterior free wind velocity, the angle at which the wind strikes the window, and the location and size of the windows.

Rooms that only have one opening in one wall have average velocities of 3.3 to 4.7% of the outside air velocity, depending on the wind direction. The difference in this velocity is small between windows that vary from 30 to 100% of the wall area. For two openings placed in the same wall, average velocities are higher, 4.3 to 15.7% of the outside air velocity, because one window acts as an inlet and the other as an outlet. If perpendicular wings are added to the wall, this average velocity can be increased to 35% when the wind blows obliquely to the wall (Givoni, p. 289; Melaragno, p. 321).

When openings in a room are located in two walls, the average interior velocity is much higher because one opening will always be in a higher pressure zone than the other. The velocity is greatly influenced by the size of the openings, and the size of the smaller opening, whether inlet or outlet, controls. The wind direction also has a significant effect on

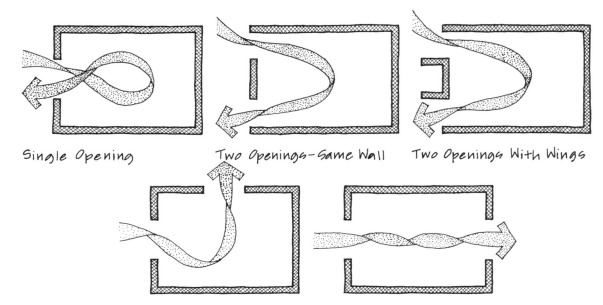

Single Opening   Two Openings—Same Wall   Two Openings With Wings

Two Openings—Adjacent Walls   Two Openings—Opposite Walls

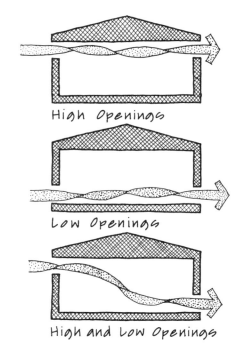

High Openings

Low Openings

High and Low Openings

	1/3	1/3	1/3
window height as a fraction of wall height			
window width as a fraction of wall width	1/3	2/3	3/3
single opening	12-14%	13-17%	16-23%
two openings in the same wall	—	22%	23%
two openings in adjacent walls	37-45%	—	—
two openings in opposite walls	35-42%	37-51%	47-65%

Average Interior Air Velocity as a Percent of the Exterior Wind Velocity for Wind Direction Perpendicular to and 45° to the Opening

interior velocity. Average velocities range from 32 to 65% of the exterior velocity.

The location of the openings and interior partitions in both plan and section influence the route of the air flow through the room. Therefore, air velocity varies within the room (Melaragno, p. 326). It is important that openings be located so that air moves past the occupants to be cooled. If the openings are all near the ceiling or all near the floor, the maximum velocity won't occur in the occupied zone, usually 1 to 6 feet above the floor. If the openings are midheight in the wall or if some are high and some are low, then higher velocities will occur in the occupied zone.

The average interior air velocity as a percentage of the exterior wind velocity may be determined for various window sizes and locations from the table. The table is based on the work of Melaragno and Givoni and assumes the window height is one-third of the wall height.

In this **house designed for the hot/humid regions of Australia,** the major rooms have openings on both sides, and the interior partitions run parallel to the prevailing wind flow. The walls have several types of openings to accommodate different ventilation rates, wind speeds, privacy and security needs, and rain control (Saini, 1970, p. 27).

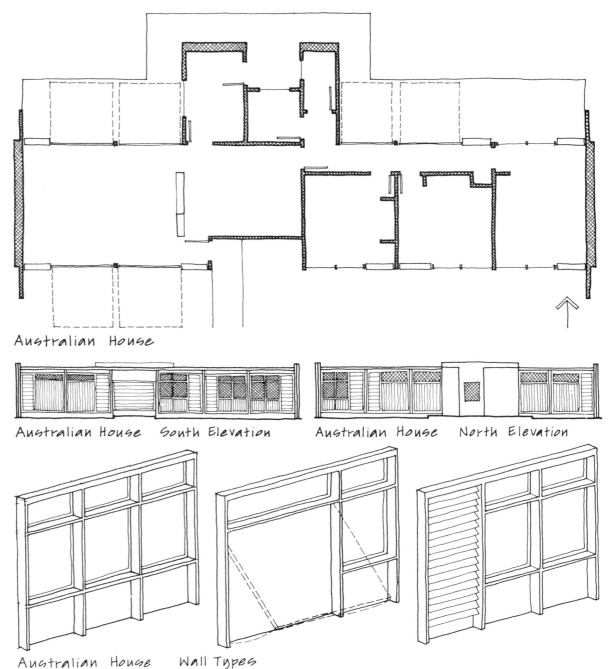

Australian House

Australian House   South Elevation

Australian House   North Elevation

Australian House   Wall Types

WINDOWS: Layers

65. *Light shelves can be used to shade view glazing, evenly distribute light, increase light levels away from windows, and reduce glare. [daylighting and cooling]*

Compared to an ordinary window of equal size and height, a window divided into upper and lower sections by a horizontal light shelf performs better in several ways. If the light shelf extends beyond the exterior surface of the glazing on sunny exposures, it can be used to shade the view glazing. At the same time, it can reflect light off its top surface through the upper glazing to the ceiling, where it is then reflected deeper into the space. The light shelf section that extends into the space also reflects light from the upper part of the window deeper into the space, while decreasing the light levels immediately adjacent to the window, thereby evening the distribution of light throughout the space. The light shelf also blocks the occupants' view of the sky, which is a potential source of glare.

The **Lockheed Building 157** in Sunnyvale, California, designed by Leo Daly, uses light shelves on both its north and south edges. The building is rectangular in plan, glazed on the north and south sides, with service functions located on the windowless east and west ends. A central atrium extends through all five floors, supplying light to the center of the building. The light shelves on the south side project out and are angled to reflect the high summer sun through the clear glazing deep into the space. The lower winter sun passes directly through the glazing and reflects off the interior light shelves. The clear upper glazing can be shaded by an exterior translucent roll-down shade. The light shelf shades the lower glazing, which is tinted and has a reflective coating. On the north side an exterior light shelf isn't needed for sun protec-

tion and the lower glazing doesn't require a reflective coating. The light shelf also houses ducts and indirect fluorescent lighting (Vonier, p. 144).

The optimum size of light shelves is governed by several considerations. They should be as low as possible, without interfering with view through the lower part of the window, so that as much light as possible reflects off their tops and penetrates deep into the space. If reducing solar gain is an important concern, the light shelves should extend beyond the building far enough to shade the view glazing. They should extend inside the building enough to block the view of the bright sky and reduce glare.

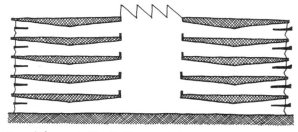

Lockheed Building 157
Sunnyvale, California

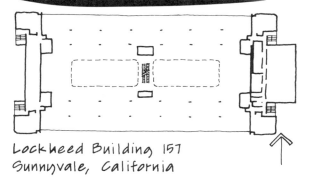

Lockheed Building 157
Sunnyvale, California

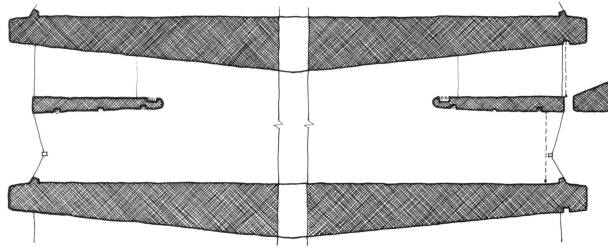

Lockheed Building 157   Sunnyvale, California

WINDOWS: Layers

66. *Shading devices can be designed to enhance daylighting. [cooling and daylighting]*

Buildings that require shaded glazing frequently also need to reduce the internal heat generated by electric lighting. However, because they cut off the windows' view of the sky dome, shading devices also reduce interior daylight levels. For example, a 6-foot horizontal overhang outside a 24-foot-deep room produces a reduction in illumination of 39% near the window and 22% near the rear wall (B. Evans, p. 62). Other studies predict reductions in illumination of 50% from exterior vertical fins at 45° to the building surface (Ander & Navvab, p. 180). Carefully designed perforations or louvers in overhangs and fins allow them to maintain the same shading characteristics but still reflect light into the space (Millet, Lakin, & Moore, p. 333). A window also "sees" more of the sky dome through the louvers, thereby increasing the daylight in the room.

Horn & Mortland used a series of louvers to form the overhang in their **school in Fresno, California.** The louvers are tightly spaced near the building to shade the high sun and loosely spaced farther away from the building to shade the low sun. In addition to admitting diffuse radiation, the open overhang also allows the circulation of air within the shading device itself, reducing heat transfers from it to the interior spaces (Olgyay & Olgyay, p. 105).

Louvers should be light in color, as they are in Aalto's **Library at Seinäjoki,** to reflect a large proportion of the diffuse light into the space (Dunster, p. 51). Because light reflected from shading devices is a potential source of glare, they should be carefully located to avoid the occupants' field of view.

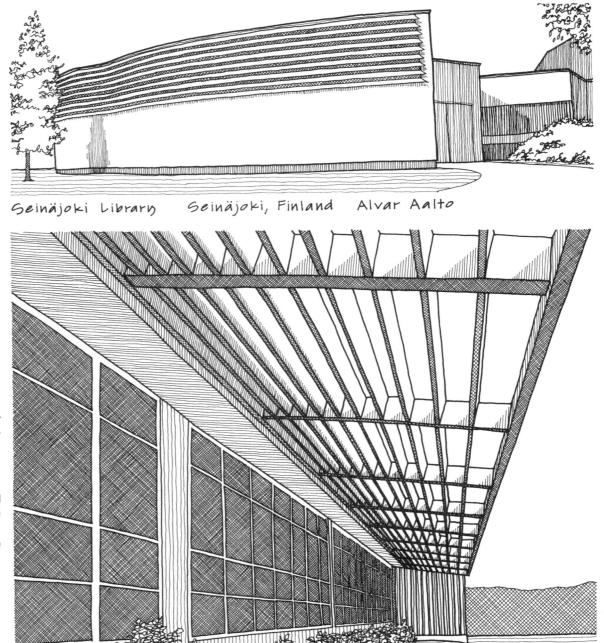

Seinäjoki Library   Seinäjoki, Finland   Alvar Aalto

Sunshine School   Fresno, California   Horn & Mortland

WINDOWS: Layers

67. A layer of movable insulation can be placed over windows to reduce heat loss at night. [heating]

Windows are usually the weakest link in the building envelope in terms of heat loss during cold weather. Heat flows out through a double glazed window ten times faster, or more, than it does through a well-insulated wall. But because it is desirable to have large windows for admitting solar radiation during the day and because the most effective window-insulating systems are opaque, the question of how to store the window insulation during the day becomes an important design consideration. While there seems to be an almost infinite variety of movable insulation schemes (Shurcliff, 1980), there are only a few conceptual design decisions that must be made at the schematic level. The two most important are whether the insulation should be in large rigid panels or flexible coverings made of small rigid pieces or membranes, and whether the insulation should be located outside, inside, or within the plane of the glazing.

Rigid panels, which require the most storage space, can be completely removed and stored in racks, hinged at the top or bottom, or mounted on sliding rails. The economic benefit of window insulation can be increased if it is usable not only when it is in the closed position, but also when it is open. An example of this is the **trombe wall shutter** which serves as a reflecting surface to increase the solar radiation collected. Rigid panels may be used in the plane of the windows like sliding pocket doors or broken into **louvers** as they are for the glazing in a sloped ceiling. The louvers may be adjusted to reflect light to the thermal mass without causing glare (Wright & Andrejko, p. 55).

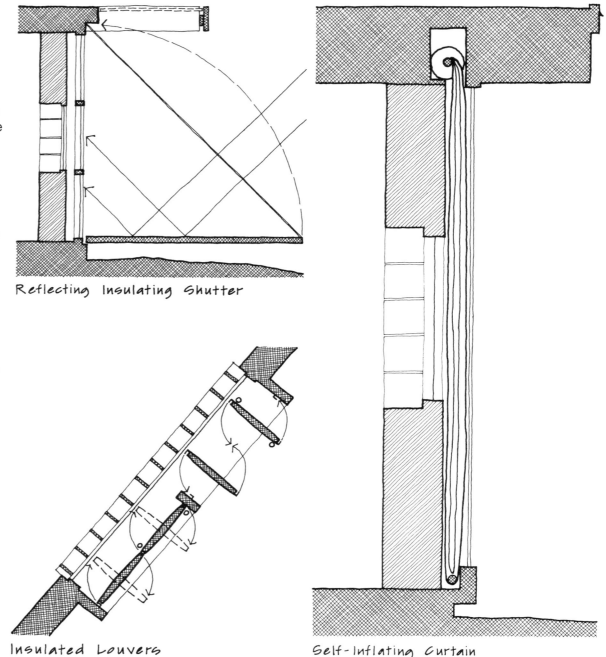

Reflecting Insulating Shutter

Insulated Louvers

Self-Inflating Curtain

Flexible covers take much less storage area than rigid covers and may be motorized and automatically closed at night and opened during the day. The trombe wall uses a **self-inflating curtain** made of several reflective layers recessed in a ceiling cavity. It is frequently simpler and less expensive to insulate several sections of glazing together than to treat each window separately.

The average R-value of a window over a 24-hour period can be determined from the graph. Find the R-value of the glass on the vertical axis and move horizontally to intersect the diagonal line corresponding to the R-value of the movable insulation and the period of operation. Then drop vertically to the horizontal axis to determine the average R-value of the window over 24 hours.

Movable insulation varies in thickness depending on R-value but varies from about ¼″ for roll-down curtains with an R of 4, to 2 to 3″ for multilayer curtains with an R of 9, to rigid boards with an R of about 4 per inch of thickness.

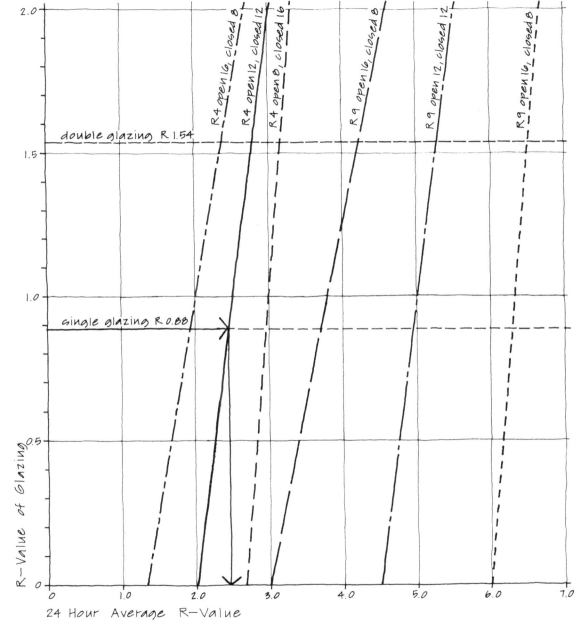

24 Hour Average R-Value of Glazing and Insulation

WINDOWS: Layers

68. *A layer can be created outside the window wall to shade the glazing and reduce solar heat gain. [cooling]*

Exterior shading devices can be either horizontal, vertical, or a combination of horizontal and vertical called "egg crates." Horizontal shades, like the overhangs on the **Radbill building,** by Louis Kahn, provide effective shading when the sun altitude is high. The depth of the device determines the length of the shadow on the window wall. In the Radbill building, the depth of the overhangs varies with the height of the glazing. They are deep on the ground floor, where the glass extends from just above the floor to the ceiling; and they are short on the top floor, where the sill heights are relatively high. The overhangs are punctured by flue tiles to let reflected light penetrate the glazing (Olgyay & Olgyay, p. 100).

The sun is higher in the summer than in the winter, so horizontal shades can be proportioned to shade in the summer but admit sun in the winter to help heat the building. Because the sun's movement is symmetrical around June 21, south-facing horizontal shades that shade the glazing in hot months (August and September) will also shade in cooler months (March and April) when the sun might be welcome. This problem can be solved by making the shades seasonally adjustable, like canvas awnings. Deciduous vines make effective shades since they are bare in the cool spring but have dense foliage throughout the hot summer and early fall.

The **Price Tower,** in Bartlesville, Oklahoma, by Frank Lloyd Wright, uses both horizontal and adjustable vertical shades, depending upon orientation. Vertical shades are effective when the sun is low if the broad side of the vertical elements faces the sun.

Egg crates combine the advantages of both horizontal and vertical shades and are particularly effective on facades that do not face south. On the west facade of the **Millowers Building, Ahmedabad, India,** by Le Corbusier, the horizontal elements shade in the early afternoon when the sun is high and the vertical elements shade in the late afternoon when the sun is low and in the west.

Shading devices can vary in size without changing their shading characteristics, as long as the **ratio** between the depth and the spacing of the elements remains constant. An example of this is in the **Palace of Justice,** Chandigarh, India, by Le Corbusier, where the depth and spacing of the screen varies with height.

Because shading devices are in the direct sun, special care must be taken so that they do not cause glare or transfer the heat they absorb into the interior of the building.

The proper size and spacing of shading elements is a function of the orientation of the windows and the time of day and year when shading is needed. The time when shading is needed can be approximated by using Techniques 10 or 19.

Even when the glazing is totally shaded, diffused light from the sky, ground, and reflection and radiation from the shading elements

S. Radbill Building   Philadelphia, Pennsylvania   Louis I. Kahn

will contribute 20% of the total exterior solar radiation to the space in the form of light and heat (Olgyay & Olgyay, p. 71).

The size and spacing of some simple shading elements may be estimated from the graph. *Determine the period of required shade and select the curve for that period. You may use the graph to determine element size given element spacing, or vice versa. The graph for south-facing windows and horizontal louvers indicates that the windows will be shaded from 8 AM to 4 PM from June 21 to the date shown on the curve and from the date shown on the curve to June 21.*

The graph for east- and west-facing windows with horizontal louvers indicates that the window will be shaded from 8 AM to 12 PM

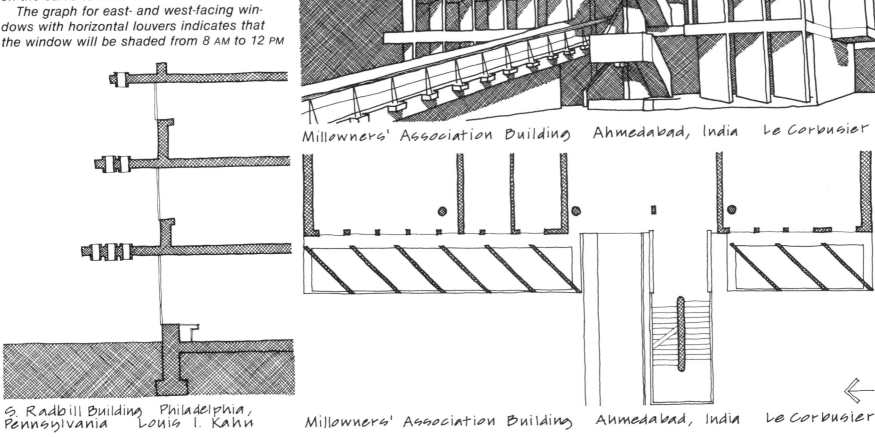

Millowners' Association Building Ahmedabad, India Le Corbusier

S. Radbill Building Philadelphia, Pennsylvania Louis I. Kahn

Millowners' Association Building Ahmedabad, India Le Corbusier

(east-facing) or 12 PM to 4 PM (west-facing) from June 21 to the date shown on the curve and from the date shown on the curve to June 21.

The graph for east- and west-facing windows with vertical fins indicates that the window will be shaded from 8 AM to 12 PM (east-facing) or 12 PM to 4 PM (west-facing) from December 21 to the date shown on the curve and from the date shown on the curve to December 21.

If the hours in the day for which shading is desired are increased or decreased, the dimensions of the shading elements for east- or west-facing windows will be substantially affected. In addition, if the fins are angled so that they are pointed north of west or east, their spacing will need to increase for a given depth.

If the shading time period is shortened, it will have no effect on the dimensions of the horizontal elements on the south-facing glazing between March 21 and September 21. From September 21 to March 21, the dimensions will be somewhat affected, especially around December 21.

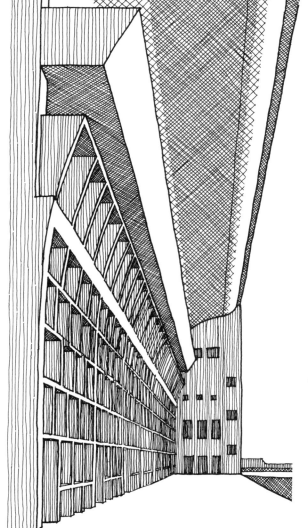

Palace of Justice
Chandigarh, India   Le Corbusier

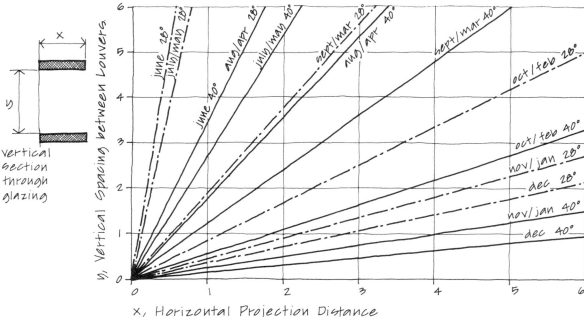

vertical section through glazing

South Facing Window, Horizontal Louver of Infinite Length, 28° & 40° N. Latitude

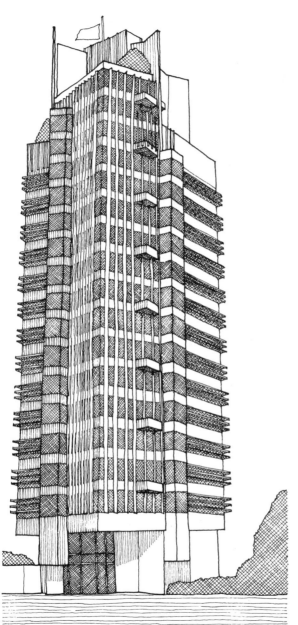

Price Tower Bartlesville, Oklahoma
Frank Lloyd Wright

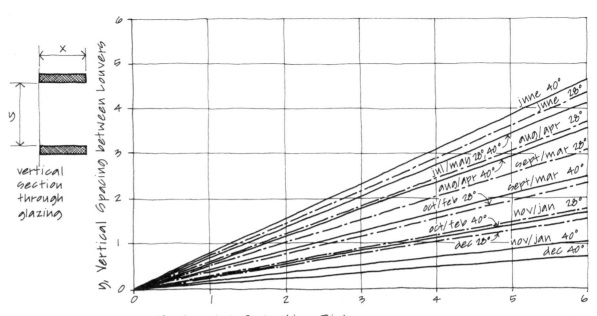

vertical
section
through
glazing

y, Vertical Spacing between Louvers

X, Horizontal Projection Distance

East or West Facing Window, Horizontal Louver of Infinite Length, 28° & 40° N. Latitude

june 40°
june 28°
aug/apr 28°
jul/may 28°, 40°
aug/apr 40°
sept/mar 28°
oct/feb 28°
sept/mar 40°
oct/feb 40°
nov/jan 28°
dec 28°
nov/jan 40°
dec 40°

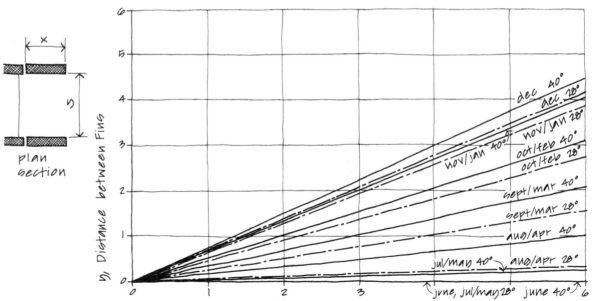

plan
section

y, Distance between Fins

X, Depth of Fin (perpendicular to building face)

East or West Facing Window, Vertical Fin of Infinite Height, 28° & 40° N. Latitude

dec 40°
dec 28°
nov/jan 40°
nov/jan 28°
oct/feb 40°
oct/feb 28°
sept/mar 40°
sept/mar 28°
aug/apr 40°
jul/may 40°
aug/apr 28°
june, jul/may 28° june 40°

PART THREE

STRATEGIES FOR SUPPLEMENTING PASSIVE SYSTEMS

As the size of buildings increases, the opportunity for total daylighting or passive solar heating and cooling decreases. This is because large buildings are more complex, it is more difficult to predict and guarantee their performance, and the criteria used to judge their performance become more restrictive. For example, the large temperature swings that might be tolerated by a few people in a small residential or commercial building might be unacceptable to the many people who occupy a large office building.

While a few solar buildings are totally passive, most use auxiliary back-up systems for peak loads. This is the case even in very efficient small buildings in relatively mild climates, because the passive solar system designed to perform under the worst conditions is significantly larger than one that performs under typical conditions.

As a result, in most design situations, an important question to answer at preliminary design stages is how much of the the heating, cooling, and lighting requirements should be satisfied by passive systems, and how much should be relegated to conventional systems.

There is also a related question about the degree to which the passive and conventional systems should replicate each other. The diagram illustrates that a building may have a range of dependence on conventional systems from complete to partial, and a range of dependence on passive systems from partial to complete. The combination of the two ranges results in a broad range of useful permutations. These can be simplified into three generic categories: (A) both conventional and passive systems are designed to perform at peak loads; (B) passive systems predominate, with a conventional back-up; (C) conventional systems predominate, but there are passive components.

The safest design approach is (A), a conventional system capable of meeting the entire heating, cooling, and lighting load with a complete passive system to carry those loads whenever it can. While safest, it is also the most expensive in terms of initial construction costs. Therefore the designer usually tries to reduce the redundancy in the systems by tending towards options (B) or (C). Since this book is mostly concerned with passive systems, the emphasis of Part Three is shown in the dotted zone—using conventional systems to supplement substantially complete passive systems.

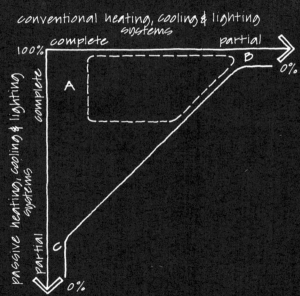

Part Three doesn't describe in any detail the conventional systems used to supplement the passive systems. Instead, it outlines some strategies for solving problems that passive systems frequently pose. These problems include achieving high illumination levels away from windows and under changing exterior lighting conditions, enhancing the building's ability to store heat and cold, and moving heat and cold from one area to another. The strategies are more general in nature than those in Part Two, and they don't attempt to supply sizing rules of thumb. Part Three is meant to be a general introduction to how passive systems can be supplemented, at a level that is appropriate for the scheming phase in the design process. It is important to realize that if completely conventional systems are anticipated, especially for large buildings, their influence on the form and organization of the building might be much more important at this design stage.

In any case, passive systems have an impact on the role of conventional heating, cooling, and lighting systems in buildings. Daylighting strategies tend to call for more external skin area, so large buildings may be less strongly dominated by internal loads. Because of the more extensive glass areas, the thermal loads at the skin, which are usually offset by conventional heating and cooling systems, can be greater. The need to get windows high in the wall can result in greater floor-to-floor heights, resulting in more air to condition and the loss of the dropped ceiling in which to place mechanical equipment.

Night ventilation of mass strategies calls for storing heat in the building during the day and removing it at night. As a consequence, the peak electrical loads that frequently occur in the afternoons on hot days, when internal gains and skin gain coincide, can be reduced, and conventional refrigeration loads can be smaller. Because air is used as a heat transfer medium at night in passive ventilation systems, conventional air systems, rather than water-cooling systems, frequently are more compatible with night ventilation schemes. The need to expose the thermal mass may result in the loss of a dropped ceiling and exposure of mechanical equipment.

Daytime ventilation schemes may eliminate the fresh air ventilation requirements normally met by conventional systems. Spaces are open and connected to each other for any return air requirements.

Since solar-heating strategies frequently result in more hot air in one location than can be used and it is transferred by ducts to cooler areas, conventional systems that use air to transfer heat may be more compatible with solar systems than those that use water.

The strategies in Part Three fall into two groups: those that affect the electric lighting system and those that affect the heating, ventilation, and air conditioning systems.

The lighting strategies (69 and 70) address the questions of how electric lights should be arranged to facilitate switching so that they won't be used unnecessarily and how daylight can be be used to meet most lighting requirements, with electric lights used only for special jobs.

Two of the remaining strategies (Strategies 71 and 72) suggest methods for extending the thermal storage capacity of buildings and improving the performance of the buildings' existing thermal storage. The last two strategies (73 and 74) suggest how heat and cold can be transferred from where they aren't needed to where they are, and how waste heat and cold can be recycled.

These supplemental system strategies shouldn't be seen as the final step in design. Rather, they should be regarded as just one more item on the schematic design checklist, to be accounted for before proceeding to the next level of detail in passive considerations.

ELECTRIC LIGHTING: Tasks

69. *Daylight can be used for ambient lighting and electric task lighting for localized, high illumination requirements.*

The farther one moves from the window, the more difficult it becomes to maintain the daylight illumination levels required for some tasks. When those tasks are localized, like desk work, the daylight can be supplemented with electric lighting located near the task and under the control of the user. This is an effective combination because daylight can still be used in large sections of the building that are distant from the window, where ambient light level requirements for talking or moving about may be lower. People can also adjust their light levels to suit their tasks and their proximity to the window, sometimes using daylight only and sometimes using a combination of daylight and electric light.

Aalto took this approach in the **Mt. Angel library** in Oregon. He put the major reading area in the center of the building directly under the skylight, where the illumination is highest, but also provided individually controlled desk lamps along the counter for use when the reading tasks are particularly difficult or when sky conditions reduce the available daylight.

Library   Mt. Angel, Oregon   Alvar Aalto

ELECTRIC LIGHTING: Layers

70. *Electric lights can be layered parallel to the window plane so that individual rows can be switched on as needed.*

Whether daylighting is used to meet task lighting conditions or ambient lighting within the daylit zone, there is a decrease in illumination as one moves away from the opening. As sky conditions change and less light is available from the sky, conditions within the zone change, with the areas farthest from the windows becoming darker sooner. If the electric lighting is layered parallel to the window plane, then lights can be turned on in the areas that need additional light and left off in areas that do not. The lighting can be controlled by a photosensitive cell so that it is automatically switched on or off when daylighting reaches a certain level or continuously dimmed so that electric lighting supplies just the supplemental light required to meet the overall illumination requirements (Sain, p. 365).

The **Central Lincoln PUD** office building in Newport, Oregon, designed by Moreland/Unruh/Smith, is daylit from the exterior sides and through a central atrium covered by a south-facing clerestory. The electric lighting system includes user-controlled task lights at each desk and indirect fluorescent lights suspended from the ceiling in rows running parallel to the windows and the atrium. The fluorescent lights are dimmer-controlled, so that they automatically adjust to available exterior illumination and maintain the minimum desirable ambient light level of 30 footcandles.

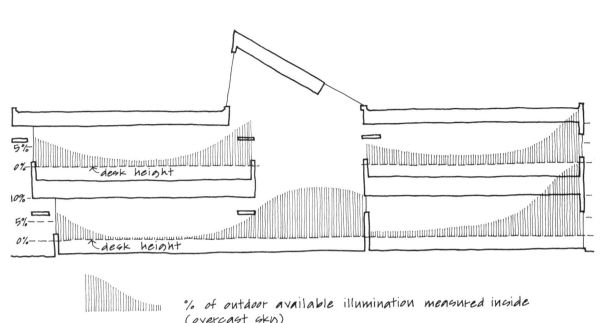

% of outdoor available illumination measured inside (overcast sky)

Central Lincoln P.U.D.　Newport, Oregon　Moreland, Unruh, Smith

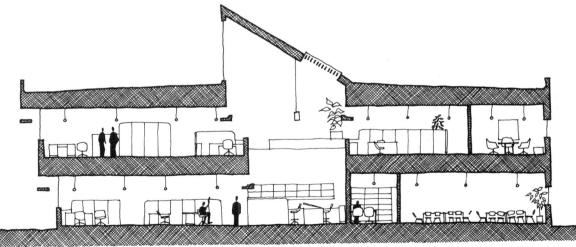

Central Lincoln P.U.D.　Newport, Oregon　Moreland, Unruh, Smith

STORAGE OF HEAT AND COLD:
Rock Beds

71. *Rock beds can be used to increase the amount of heat or cold that can be effectively stored.*

In passive solar heating and cooling systems, it is frequently advantageous to increase the thermal storage beyond what is available in the building's structure. Rock beds are a means of enlarging the thermal mass of the building and thereby increasing its ability to store energy. In a heating system, air is drawn by fan and ducts from a location where it is hot, like the top of a sunspace or in front of a trombe wall, through a bed of rocks. Heat is given off to the rocks and the air is recirculated to a location in the hot space to collect more heat. At night, when heat is needed, air from the occupied space is drawn through the rock bed, where it picks up heat and is distributed back to the occupied space. The rock bed can be located under a concrete floor that will be heated by the bed and in turn heat the space. The fans required to charge and discharge the rock bed are frequently part of the conventional HVAC system. The size of the rock bed is a function of the input air temperature, heat storage requirements, rock size, and the air flow rate (Balcomb, Jones, et al., p. 192).

Rock beds for cooling are similar to those for heating except that the source of cool air is frequently outside the building. In climates that experience a large diurnal temperature swing, cool outside air can be drawn through the bed at night. In hot arid climates the rock bed may be cooled by evaporation (Yellott, p. 767).

In the **Princeton Professional Park** in Princeton, New Jersey, designed by Harrison Fraker, an under-floor rock bed is used to store both

Princeton Professional Park   Princeton, New Jersey
Princeton Energy Group

heat and cold. During the winter day, hot air is drawn from the top of the solar-heated atrium into an under-floor rock bed, where the air gives off its heat to the rocks and is returned to the atrium to be reheated. At night, heat is transferred from the rock bed to the space by two modes: heating the floor slab directly by conduction and warming the air by an active forced air system.

In the summer at night the metal roof is cooled by radiation to the night sky and by evaporation of a water spray. Air from the rock bed is blown under the metal roof, losing its heat to the roof, and then recirculated through the rock bed, cooling the rocks. During the day air from the space is circulated through the rock bed to cool it (*Progressive Architecture*, 4/83, p. 96).

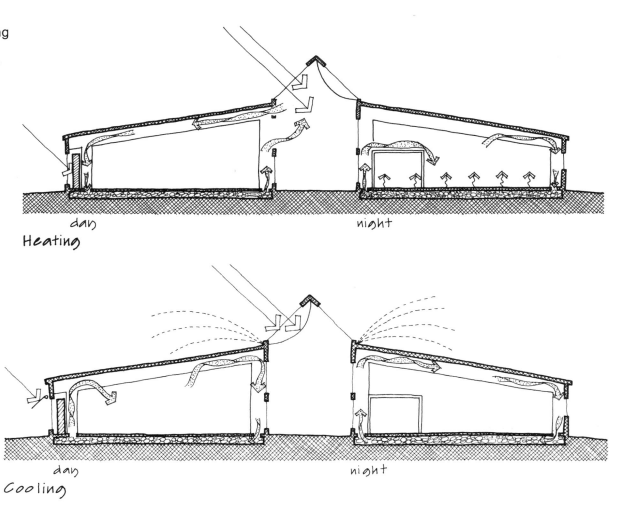

STORAGE OF HEAT AND COLD:
Mechanical Ventilation

72. *Mechanical ventilation can be used to insure adequate air movement past the building's mass, thereby improving its cooling potential.*

Schemes for night ventilation of mass are designed to store heat during the day in the mass of the building and lose heat to the cool ventilating air at night. Because the rate of air movement is frequently low, the flow poorly distributed, and the amount of mass area limited, the cooling potential in passive systems is limited. Therefore, using fans to increase the rate of air movement past the mass increases the amount of heat that can be removed during the night.

Mechanical night ventilation of thermal mass is an important cooling strategy in the **Bateson Building** in Sacramento, California, designed by the office of the State Architect. It satisfies about 65% of the building's cooling load. The building uses extensive shading and daylighting and an interior atrium to reduce the magnitude of the cooling load. The night ventilation system works by pulling cool outside air down the ventilation shaft at night and distributing it to each space by the HVAC system. It then picks up heat from the structure and is exhausted to the outside. The major mass area is in the ceiling, where the precast concrete double T's are left exposed. Daylighting is supplemented by indirect pedestal lights that light the ceiling and task lights at individual work stations. Sound-absorbing material is suspended vertically between the legs of the T's. The thermal mass of the building is supplemented with a rock bed storage system (*Progressive Architecture*, 8/81, p. 76).

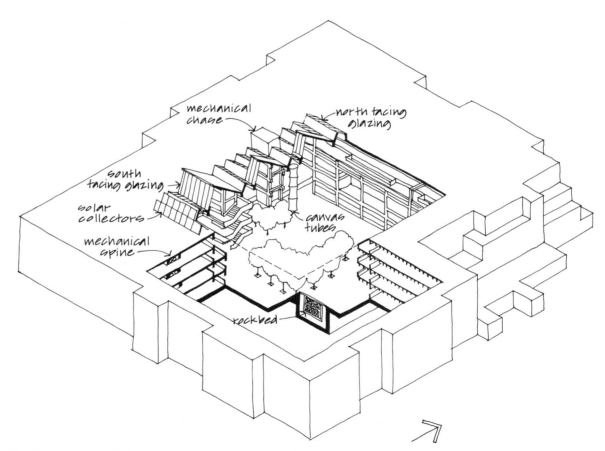

Bateson Building   Sacramento, California   Office of the State Architect

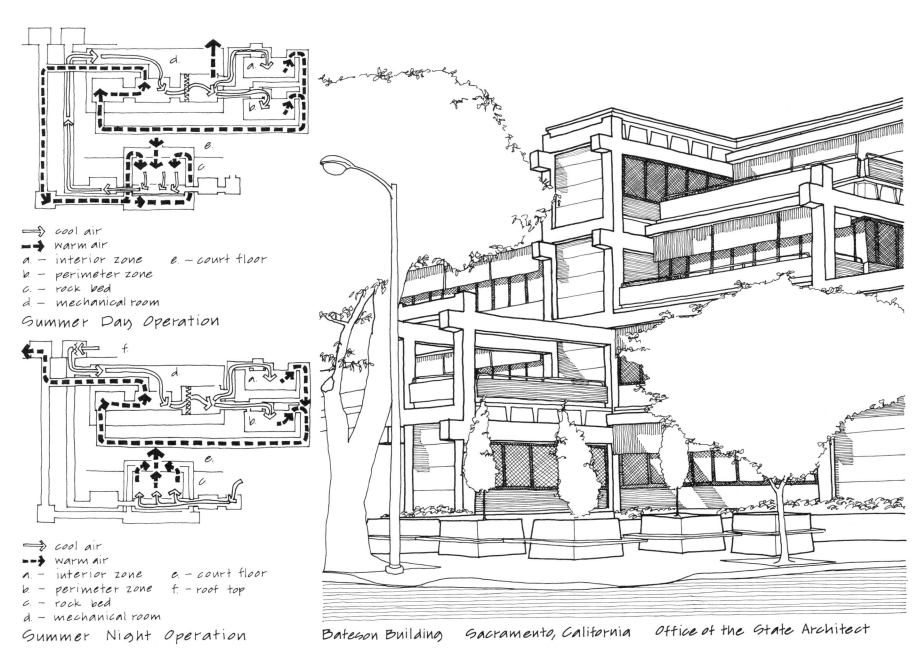

cool air ⟹

warm air ⟹

a. – interior zone   e. – court floor

b. – perimeter zone

c. – rock bed

d. – mechanical room

Summer Day Operation

cool air ⟹

warm air ⟹

a. – interior zone   e. – court floor

b. – perimeter zone   f. – roof top

c. – rock bed

d. – mechanical room

Summer Night Operation

Bateson Building   Sacramento, California   Office of the State Architect

DISTRIBUTION SYSTEMS:
Heat Exchangers

73. *Heat exchangers can be used to reclaim heat and cold from the ventilation air.*

In closed building design strategies in which heat loss and gain through the building skin are carefully controlled, heating or cooling incoming fresh air becomes a major energy user in the building. With ventilation rates below one air change per hour, there is a danger of air pollution within the building as a result of chemicals and radiation emitted by building materials. One way to reduce the energy used to heat or cool incoming air without reducing its volume below safe limits is to use the heat or cold escaping from the building to heat or cool the incoming air.

Fan powered air-to-heat exchangers are frequently used in ducted systems. Air exhausted from the building is passed by or through a series of thin metal planes, giving off its heat or cold, and incoming air is passed by or through the same planes, picking up heat or cold. Air-to-air heat exchangers can recapture 70 to 90% of the outgoing heat or cold (Shurcliff, 1981, p. 12.02).

Although this is not as efficient, ventilation air can also be heated or cooled by bringing it past exterior building surfaces like windows that are either hot or cold. Aalto used this approach at the **Tuberculosis Sanatorium** in Paimio, where air is brought in between layers of glass to individual rooms. Heat being lost through the glass is used to heat the incoming air (Fleig, p. 78).

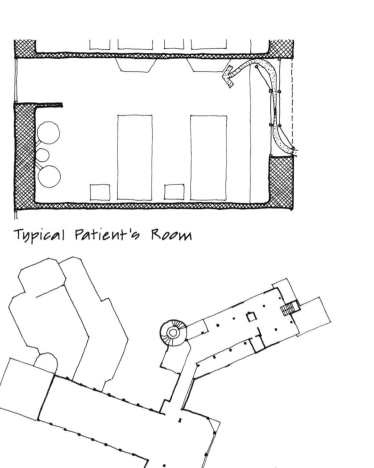

Typical Patient's Room

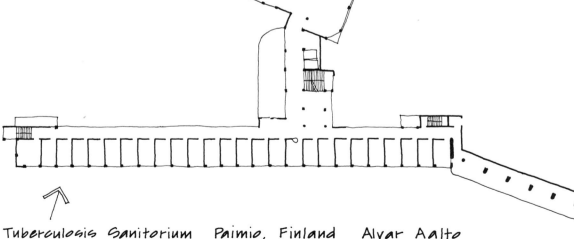

Tuberculosis Sanitorium Paimio, Finland Alvar Aalto

DISTRIBUTION SYSTEMS:
Moving Heat and Cold

74. *Ducts and plenums can be used to move heat to cool parts of building and cold to hot parts of the building.*

Heat sources like the sun and heat sinks like the night sky are not equally accessible to all parts of the building. Thus some buildings need to have heat transported to cooler areas in the heating season and cold transported to hot areas during the cooling season.

Internal load-dominated buildings with constant cooling loads, and therefore an excess of heat, in cold climates frequently have some exposures that require heat that can be supplied from overheated areas in the building.

The central atruim in the **Bateson Building** in Sacramento, California *(Progressive Architecture, 8/81, p 76)*, is used primarily to supply light to the building interior. Because it is not conditioned but is used as a circulation and meeting space, it must supply its own heating, which it does by capturing solar radiation through its south-facing clerestories. Because the space is tall, the hot air tends to collect at the top of the space. The hot air is circulated from the top of the space to the bottom, where the people are, through canvas ducts hung from the ceiling. Each duct has a fan at its lower end. In the summer, cool night air is drawn down ventilating shafts located above the roof to cool the mass of the atrium, and then the warmed air is released through skylight vents.

In the **Conservation Center,** Society for the Protection of New Hampshire Forests, Concord, New Hampshire, designed by Banwel, White and Arnold, sunlight is collected through south-facing windows and clerestories. Solar energy that isn't immediately stored in the building's mass, water tubes, or phase change materials heats the air that rises to the top of the clerestory. The hot air is drawn, by a fan located below the clerestory, through a roof plenum down the rear masonry wall and through the concrete floor, losing its heat. In the summer, overheated air is vented from the clerestory to the outside *(Progressive Architecture, 4/83, p. 86)*.

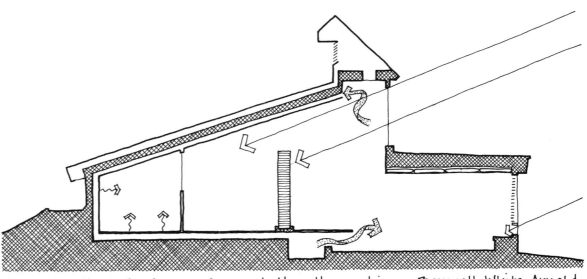

Conservation Center   Concord, New Hampshire   Banwell, White, Arnold

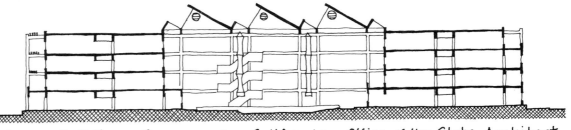

Bateson Building   Sacramento, California   Office of the State Architect

GLOSSARY

AIR CHANGES
A measure of the air exchange in a building due to infiltration or ventilation. One air change occurs when the building's entire volume of air has been replaced.

AMBIENT TEMPERATURE
Surrounding air temperature, as in a room or around a building.

ATTACHED SUNSPACE
A room that doubles as a solar collector; also called *attached greenhouse, solarium.* The term *attached* also implies a space that shares one common wall with the associated building.

AUXILIARY HEAT
Heat delivered to a building by conventional systems to supplement solar heat.

AZIMUTH
The angle of the sun, as seen in plan; also, the orientation of a building. An azimuth of zero describes a glazing or wall that faces due south.

BTU (BRITISH THERMAL UNIT)
A unit of heat; specifically, the heat needed to raise the temperature of one pound of water by 1°F.

CLO
A measure of the insulating value of clothing. For example, .3 Clo is typical for light summer clothing; .8 is typical for heavy winter clothing.

CONDITIONED AND UNCONDITIONED SPACES
Conditioned spaces need air treatment such as heat addition, heat removal, moisture removal, or pollution removal. Unconditioned spaces do not need such air conditioning, and no effort is made to control infiltration.

CONDUCTANCE
A measure of the rate of heat flow between two surfaces, measured in Btu per hour per degrees Fahrenheit, per square foot of material that separates the two surfaces (Btu per hr. per F° per sq. ft.).

CONDUCTION
The transfer of heat through a static medium, usually a solid such as concrete.

CONDUCTIVITY
See *thermal conductivity.*

CONTRAST
A qualitative perception of the difference between two elements in the visual field. The subjective assessment of the difference in appearance of two parts of a field of view seen simultaneously or successively.

CONVECTION
Heat transferred between a surface and an adjacent fluid (usually air or water) by the circulation of that fluid, induced by a temperature differential.

DAYLIGHT FACTOR
The proportion of outdoor illumination that arrives at an interior work plane.

DELTA T (ΔT)
A difference in temperature, usually referring to the difference between indoor and outdoor temperatures.

DIFFUSE RADIATION
The component of solar radiation that has been scattered by atmospheric particles. Diffuse radiation is assumed to be evenly distributed throughout the sky dome.

DIRECT GAIN
The transmission of sunlight directly into the space to be heated, where it is converted to heat by absorption on the interior surfaces.

DIRECT RADIATION
The component of solar radiation that comes directly from the sun without being diffused or reflected.

EXTERNALLY REFLECTED COMPONENT OF DAYLIGHT FACTOR
The portion of the daylight factor that is contributed by external reflected surfaces such as the ground and adjacent buildings.

FOOTCANDLE
A measure of illumination; specifically, the amount of direct light from one candle falling on a square foot of surface one foot away.

FOOT LAMBERT
A measure of illumination including factors of reflection, transmission, and emission, from one candle, falling on a square foot of surface one foot away.

GLARE
A very bright light or a high contrast of light making it uncomfortable or difficult to see.

GLAZING
Transparent or translucent materials, usually glass or plastic, used to cover an opening without impeding the admission of heat and light.

HEAT CAPACITY
A measure of the ability of an element of thermal storage mass to store heat in units of Btu per F°.

HEAT GAIN
The gross amount of heat that is introduced into a space, whether from incoming radiation or from internal sources such as occupants, lights, and equipment.

HEATING DEGREE DAYS (DD)
The sum of the differences between a selected interior temperature and the daily mean outdoor temperatures. Only positive differences are counted; that is, when the outdoor mean is less than the base temperature. The daily mean is computed as the mean of the daily minimum and maximum temperatures.

HEAT LOAD
The net heat loss (in Btu) from a building for a designated time period.

HEAT LOSS
The gross amount of heat that leaves a space, either by heat flow through the building envelope or by air infiltration.

HVAC
Mechanical systems for Heating, Ventilating, and Air Conditioning.

HYBRID SYSTEM
A solar heating or cooling system that combines passive and active elements.

INDIRECT GAIN
The transfer of solar heat into the space to be heated from a collector that is coupled to the space by an uninsulated, conductive, or convective medium; for example, thermal storage walls and roof ponds.

INFILTRATION
Air exchange between interior spaces and the outdoors, resulting in heat loss or gain.

INSOLATION
The total amount of direct, diffuse, and reflected solar radiation that strikes a surface. Insolation is usually measured in Btu per sq. ft. per hour or per day.

INSULATION
Low mass material with high thermal resistance used to slow the transfer of heat by conduction.

INTERNAL HEAT GAIN
Heat generated inside the building by sources other than the space-heating equipment, usually by appliances, lights, and people.

INTERNALLY REFLECTED COMPONENT OF DAYLIGHT FACTOR
The portion of the daylight factor contributed by internal reflecting surfaces such as walls, floor, and ceiling.

INTERNAL SOURCES
The sources of internal heat gain other than the space-heating equipment, such as appliances, lights, and people.

ISOLATED GAIN
The transfer of heat into a space from a collector that is thermally isolated either by physical separation or insulation. Examples include convective loop collectors and attached sunspaces with an insulated common wall.

LATENT HEAT
A change in heat content that occurs without a corresponding change in temperature, usually accompanied by a change of state, as when water vapor in the air condenses.

LOAD
The demand for energy required at any moment to compensate for the difference between existing outdoor conditions and desired indoor conditions.

LOAD COLLECTOR RATIO (LCR)
The ratio of the building load coefficient (BLC) to the collection area. LCR is an expression of the relationship between energy conservation and solar gain and can be used to compare buildings within the same locality.

MASONRY
Concrete block, brick, adobe, stone, concrete, and other similar materials.

MASS-AREA-TO-GLAZING-AREA RATIO
The ratio of the surface area of massive elements in a direct gain building to the total solar collection area. Massive elements include all floors, walls, ceilings, and other high density interior objects.

MET
A measure of the heat produced by a sedentary person. One met unit = 18.4 Btu per hr. per sq. ft.

NATURAL CONVECTION
Heat transfer between a surface and adjacent fluid (usually air or water), by the circulation of the fluid induced by temperature differences only and not by mechanical means.

NIGHT SKY RADIATION
A reversal of the daylight insolation principle. Just as the sun radiates energy during the day through the void of space, so heat energy can travel unhindered at night, from the earth's surface back into space. On a clear night the earth, like any other warm object, can cool itself by radiating long-wave heat energy to the cooler sky. On a cloudy night, the cloud cover acts as an insulator and prevents the heat from traveling to the cooler sky.

OPAQUE
Not able to transmit light; for example, unglazed walls.

PASSIVE SYSTEM
A system that uses nonmechanical means to satisfy heating or cooling loads.

REFERENCE NONSOLAR BUILDING
A building similar to a solar building but with an energy-neutral wall in place of the solar wall and with a constant indoor reference temperature. Used as a reference for assessing the performance of solar buildings.

RELATIVE HUMIDITY
The percentage of the amount of water vapor in the atmosphere relative to the maximum amount of water vapor that can be held by the air at a given temperature.

ROCK STORAGE SYSTEM
A solar energy storage system in which the collected heat or cold is stored in a rock bin for later use. This type of storage can be used in an active, hybrid, or even passive system.

ROOF POND SYSTEM
An indirect gain heating and cooling system in which the mass, which is water in plastic bags, is located on the roof of the space to be heated or cooled. A roof pond system absorbs solar radiation for heating in the winter and radiates heat to the night sky for cooling in the summer.

R-VALUE
A measure of the thermal resistance of a building element; the reciprocal of the U-value. See *thermal resistance.*

SEMI-ENCLOSED SUNSPACE
A sunspace that shares three common walls with the associated building.

SENSIBLE HEAT
Heat that results in a change in air temperature, in contrast with latent heat.

SKY COMPONENT OF DAYLIGHT FACTOR
The portion of the daylight factor contributed by luminance from the sky, excluding direct sunlight.

SKY LUMINANCE DISTRIBUTION— THE C.I.E. STANDARD OVERCAST SKY
A completely overcast sky for which the ratio of luminance at an altitude θ above the horizon to the luminance at the zenith is assumed to be $(1 + 2 \sin \theta)/3$.

SOLAR ABSORPTANCE
The fraction of incident solar radiation that is absorbed by a surface. The radiation not absorbed is reflected.

SOLAR APERTURE
That portion of the solar wall covered by glazing. The orientation of the opening should be within 30° of south to be considered a solar aperture.

SOLAR RADIATION
Radiation emitted by the sun including infrared radiation, ultraviolet radiation, and visible light.

SOLAR TIME
Time of day adjusted so that the sun is due south at noon.

SPECIFIC HEAT
The amount of heat in Btu's required to raise the temperature of one pound of a material 1°F.

STRATIFICATION
The tendency of fluids, like air and water, to form layers when unevenly heated. The warmer fluid rises to the top of the available enclosure, and the cooler fluid drops to the bottom.

SUNSPACE
See *attached sunspace.*

THERMAL BREAK (THERMAL BARRIER)
An element of low heat conductivity placed within a composite construction in such a way as to reduce the flow of heat.

THERMAL CONDUCTIVITY
A measure of the ease with which heat flows in a material by conduction, specifically, the heat flow rate in Btu per inch of material thickness, square foot of material area, and degree of temperature difference. (Btu per hr. per ft. per F°.)

THERMAL RADIATION
Energy transfer in the form of electromagnetic waves from a body by virtue of its temperature, including infrared radiation, ultraviolet radiation, and visible light.

THERMAL RESISTANCE
A measure of the insulation value or resistance to heat conduction of building elements or materials; specifically, the reciprocal of the thermal conductance, also called *R-value.*

THERMAL STORAGE MASS
High density building elements such as masonry or water in containers, designed to absorb solar heat during the day for release later when heat is needed.

THERMOCIRCULATION
The circulation of a fluid by convection. For example, the convection from a warm zone (sunspace or trombe-wall air space) to a cool zone through openings in a common wall.

TROMBE WALL
A masonry thermal storage wall placed between the solar aperture and the heated space. Heat is transferred into the space by conduction through the masonry and, if vents are provided, by natural convection.

U-VALUE (COEFFICIENT OF HEAT TRANSFER)
A measure of heat flow, specifically, the number of Btu's that flow through one square foot of building skin, in one hour, when there is a

1 °F difference in temperature between the inside and outside air, under steady state conditions. The U-value is the reciprocal of the resistance or R-value.

VENTILATION (NATURAL)
Air flow through and within a space stimulated by either the distribution of pressure gradients around a building or thermal forces caused by temperature gradients between indoor and outdoor air.

WATER WALL
A thermal storage wall of water in containers placed between the solar aperture and the heated space. Heat is transferred into the space by conduction and convection through the water.

WORKING PLANE (REFERENCE PLANE)
The horizontal work surface, usually at about 30 to 36 inches from the floor, at which illumination is specified and measured.

BIBLIOGRAPHY

Al-Azzaui, Subhi Hussein. "Oriental Houses in Iraq." Paul Oliver, ed. *Shelter In Society,* New York: Frederick A. Praeger, 1969.

American Society of Heating, Refrigerating and Air-Conditioning Engineers, Inc. (ASHRAE). *Handbook of Fundamentals.* New York, 1972.

Ander, G.D., and M. Navvab. "Daylight Impacts of Fenestration Controls," *Proceedings of the 8th National Passive Solar Conference,* American Solar Energy Society, 1983.

Arens, E., P. McNall, R. Gonzalez, L. Berglund, and L. Zeren. "A New Bioclimatic Chart for Passive Solar Design," *Proceedings of the 5th National Passive Solar Conference,* American Section of the International Solar Energy Society, 1980.

Aynsley, R.M., W. Melbourne, and B.J. Vickery. *Architectural Aerodynamics.* London: Applied Science, 1977.

Balcomb, J.D. "Conservation and Solar Guidelines," *Proceedings of the 8th National Passive Solar Conference,* American Solar Energy Society, 1983.

Balcomb, J.D., D. Barley, R. McFarland, J. Perry Jr., W. Wray, and S. Noll. *Passive Solar Design Handbook* (Vol. 2). Washington, DC: U.S. Department of Energy, 1980.

Balcomb, J.D., R.W. Jones, ed., C.E. Kosiewicz, G.S. Lazarus, R.D. McFarland, and W.O. Wray. *Passive Solar Design Handbook* (Vol. 3). New York: American Solar Energy Society, 1983.

Balcomb, J. D., and K. Yamaguchi. "Heat Distribution by Natural Convention," *Proceedings of the 8th National Passive Solar Conference,* American Solar Energy Society, 1983.

Brown, G.Z., and B. Novitski. "A Design Methodology Based on Climate Characteristics," *Proceedings of the 6th National Passive Solar Conference,* American Section of the International Solar Energy Society, 1981.

Brown, G.Z., and J.S. Reynolds. "Deadwood Oregon Community Center and Firehall," *Proceedings of 1981 Passive and Hybrid Solar Energy Program Update Conference,* Washington, DC, 1981.

Brown, G.Z., J. Reynolds, and M.S. Ubbelohde. *INSIDEOUT: Design Procedures for Passive Environmental Technologies.* New York: John Wiley & Sons, 1982.

Butti, K., and J. Perlin. *A Golden Thread: 2500 Years of Solar Architecture and Technology.* New York: Van Nostrand Reinhold, 1980.

Changery, M.J., W.T. Hodge, and J.V. Ramsdell. *Index–Summarized Wind Data.* U.S. Department of Commerce, National Oceanic and Atmospheric Administration; and Battelle, Pacific Northwest Laboratories, BNWL-220, WIND-11, UC-60, September 1977.

Coles, A., and P. Jackson. "A Windtower House in Dubai," *Art and Archeaology Research Papers,* London, June, 1975.

Commission Internationale de l'Eclairage (CIE). *Daylight,* Publication CIE No. 16 (E-3.2). Paris, 1970.

Department of City Planning (New York). *Midtown Development. New York:* The New York Department of City Planning, 1981.

Dunster, D., ed. *Alvar Aalto,* Architectural Monographs 4. London, 1978.

Evans, B.H. *Daylighting in Architecture.* New York: McGraw-Hill, 1981.

Evans, M. *Housing, Climate and Comfort.* London: The Architectural Press, 1980.

Fleig, K., ed. *Alvar Aalto.* New York: Praeger, 1975.

Fleischnacker, P., G. Clark, and P. Giolma. "Geographical Limits for Comfort in Unassisted Roof Pond Cooled Residences," *Proceedings of the 8th National Passive Solar Conference,* American Solar Energy Society, 1983.

Flynn, J.E., and A.W. Segil. *Architectural Interior Systems.* New York: Van Nostrand Reinhold, 1970.

Fry, M., and J. Drew. *Tropical Architecturel in the Humid Zone.* New York: Van Nostrand Reinhold, 1956.

Givoni, B. *Man, Climate, and Architecture.* London: Applied Science, 1976.

Golany, G., ed. *Housing in Arid Lands.* London: Architectural Press, 1980.

Hildebrand, G. *Designing for Industry: The Architecture of Albert Kahn.* Cambridge: MIT Press, 1974.

Hitchcock, H.R. *The Architecture of H. H. Richardson and His Times.* New York: Museum of Modern Art, 1936.

_____. *In the Nature of Materials.* New York: Hawthorn Books, 1942.

Hopkinson, R.G., P. Petherbridge, and J. Longmore. *Daylighting*. London: Heinemann, 1966.

Illuminating Engineering Society of North America. *Recommended Practice of Daylighting*. New York, 1979.

Knowles, R.L. *Energy and Form: An Ecological Approach to Urban Growth*. Cambridge: MIT Press, 1974.

————. *Sun Rhythm Form*. Cambridge: MIT Press, 1981.

Koenigsberger, O.H., T. Ingersoll, A. Mayhew, and S. Szokolay. *Manual of Tropical Housing and Building, Part One: Climatic Design*. London: Longman Group, 1973.

Kusuda, T. and K. Ishii. *Hourly Solar Radiation Data for Vertical and Horizontal Surfaces on Average Days in the U.S. and Canada.* Building Science Series 96, National Bureau of Standards, 1977.

Labs, K. "Terratypes: Underground Housing for Arid Zones." In *Housing in Arid Lands,* G. Golany, ed. New York: John Wiley & Sons, 1980.

Lambeth, J., and J.D. Delap. *Solar Designing*. Fayetteville, AR: Lambeth, 1977.

Libbey-Owens-Ford. *Sun Angle Calculator*. Toledo, Ohio 1974.

Loftness, V. *Climate/Energy Graphics*. Washington, DC: Association of Collegiate Schools of Architecture, 1981.

Longmore, J. *BRS Daylight Protractors*. London: Her Majesty's Stationary Office, 1978.

Lynch, K. *Site Planning* (2nd ed.). Cambridge: MIT Press, 1971.

Mazria, E. *The Passive Solar Energy Book*. Emmaus, PA: Rodale Press, 1979.

McGuiness, W.J., B. Stein, and J.S. Reynolds. *Mechanical and Electrical Equipment for Buildings* (6th ed.). New York: John Wiley & Sons, 1980.

Melaragno, M. *Wind in Architectural and Environmental Design*. New York: Van Nostrand Reinhold, 1982.

Millet, M., J. Lakin, and J. Moore. "Light Without Heat: Daylight and Shading," *Proceedings of the International Passive and Hybrid Cooling Conference,* American Section of the International Solar Energy Society, 1981.

Myrup, L.O. "A Numerical Model of the Urban Heat Island," *Journal of Applied Meteorology, 8,* 1969.

Olgyay, A., and V. Olgyay. *Solar Control and Shading Devices*. Princeton, NJ: Princeton University Press, 1957.

Olgyay, V. *Design With Climate*. Princeton, NJ: Princeton University Press, 1963.

Packard, R.T., ed. *Architectural Graphic Standards* (7th ed.). New York: John Wiley & Sons, 1981.

Reed, R.A. "Tree Windbreaks for the Central Great Plains," *Agriculture Handbook #250,* U.S. Department of Agriculture, 1964.

Reed, R.H. "Design for Natural Ventilation in Hot Humid Weather," *Housing and Building in Hot-Humid and Hot-Dry Climates,* Building Research Advisory Board, Research Conference Report No. 5, National Research Council, National Academy of Sciences, 1953.

Rifkind, C. *A Field Guide to American Architecture*. New York: The New American Library, 1980.

Robinette, G.O. *Plants/People/and Environmental Quality*. Washington, DC: U.S. Department of Interior, National Park Service; and American Society of Landscape Architects Foundation, 1972.

Robinette, G.O., ed. *Landscape Planning for Energy Conservation*. Reston, VA: Environmental Design Press, 1977.

Sain, A.M. "Daylighting and Artificial Lighting Control," *Proceedings of the International Daylighting Conference,* Phoenix, 1983.

Saini, B.S. *Architecture in Tropical Australia,* Architectural Association Paper No. 6. New York: George Wittenborn, 1970.

————. *Building in Hot Dry Climates*. New York: John Wiley & Sons, 1980.

Sande, T.A. "Inherent Energy-Saving Features of Old Buildings." In *New Energy from Old Buildings,* D. Maddex, ed. Washington, DC: The Preservation Press, 1981.

Schoenauer, N. *Introduction to Contemporary Indigenous Housing*. Montreal: Reporter Books, 1973.

Scully, V. *Louis I. Kahn*. New York: George Braziller, 1962.

Sergeant, J. *Frank Lloyd Wright's Usonian Houses*. New York: Whitney Library of Design, 1975.

Shurcliff, W.A. *Thermal Shutters and Shades*. Andover, MA: Brick House, 1980.

————. *Air to Air Heat Exchangers for Houses*. Cambridge, MA: W.A. Shurcliff, 1981.

Smith, B.M. "Making Buildings Work as They Were Intended." In *New Energy from Old Buildings,* D. Maddex, ed. Washington, DC: The Preservation Press, 1981.

Sterling, R., J. Carmody, and G. Elnicky. *Earth Sheltered Community Design*. New York: Van Nostrand Reinhold, 1981.

United States Department of Commerce, National Oceanic and Atmospheric Administration (NOAA). *Airport Climatological Summary.* Asheville, NC: National Climatic Center.

_____. *Comparative Climate Data through 1976.* Asheville, NC: National Climatic Center, 1977.

_____. *Local Climatological Data.* Asheville, NC: National Climatic Center.

_____. *Local Climatological Data; Annual Summary with Comparative Data.* Asheville, NC: National Climatic Center.

_____. *Revised Uniform Summary of Surface Weather Observations.* Asheville, NC: National Climatic Center.

United States Department of Energy. *Predesign Energy Analysis.* DOE/CS, 0171, 1980.

Vonier, T., ed. *General Proceedings.* 1983 International Daylighting Conference, Phoenix.

Watson, D., ed. *Energy Conservation Through Building Design.* New York: McGraw-Hill, 1979.

Watson, D., and R. Glover. *Solar Control Workbook.* Washington, DC: Association of Collegiate Schools of Architecture, 1981.

Watson, D., and K. Labs. *Climatic Design.* New York: McGraw-Hill, 1983.

Wright, D., and D. Andrejko. *Passive Solar Architecture.* New York: Van Nostrand Reinhold, 1982.

Yellott, J. "Evaporative Cooling," *Proceedings of the International Passive and Hybrid Cooling Conference,* American Section of the International Solar Energy Society, 1981.

Zeren, L. "Urban and Architectural Planning in Warm, Arid Zones." In *Desert Planning,* G. Golan, ed. London: The Architectural Press, 1982.

SUBJECT INDEX

Fans, 154–155. *See also* Ventilation
Fences, 77
Floors:
    colors
        for daylighting, 122
        for solar heating, 121
    heat flow estimation, 44
    skin insulation requirements, 120
    thermal mass surfaces, 123
Fountains:
    courtyards as cold air sinks, 114
    water edges strategy, 78

Gardens, 76, 77. *See also* Landscaping; Planting
Glare:
    daylighting by reflection, 135
    reduction of, 126
    window shading devices, 141
        exterior, 144
Glass, heat flow estimation, 44. *See also* Windows
Glazing, *see* Windows

Heat exchangers, 156
Heat flow estimation, 44–45
Heat gain:
    balance point and, 52
    bioclimatic design strategies, 50
    by building type, 54
    daily heating cooling patterns, 56–61
    daylighting by reflection, 135
    electric lighting, 40
    equipment, 41
    estimation of, 48
    occupancy, 38–39
    room zoning for, 108
    see also Solar heat gain
Heating:
    bioclimatic chart approach, 34
    colors and, 121
    courtyard and room enclosure, 115
    courtyard and room zoning, 116–117
    daily generic strategies, 56–61
    direct gain solar system, 92–94
    ducts and plenums, 157
    earth sheltering strategy, 86–88
    east-west axis room arrangement, 104–105
    elongated solar gain, 80–81
    form and envelope, 43
    heat exchangers, 156
    heat loss by window size, 134
    internal heat gain estimation, 38–39

passive solar supplementation, 148–149
rock bed storage, 152–153
roofs as reflecting surfaces for solar radiation, 125
room clustering, 106
room zoning:
    for buffer areas, 110
    for internal heat gain, 108
    for temperature stratification, 109
skin insulation requirements, 120
solar heating by window size, 130–133
thermal insulation of massive storage walls, 124
thermal mass surfaces, 123
transition to cooling, 52–55
program and use, 37
roof ponds, 97
shading and, 14
solar envelope and, 68–71
solar heat gain estimation, 46–47
sunspaces, 95
topographical microclimates, 74
trombe wall strategy, 96
ventilation/infiltration, 48
vertical glazing, 89
wind breaks, 76–77
window insulation, 142–143
windows, 136–137
wind-protected, sunny exterior spaces, 75
see also Solar heating
Heat loss:
    balance point and, 52
    by building type, 55
    daily heating cooling patterns, 56–61
    earth sheltering, 86–87
    estimation of, 48
    window insulation, 142–143
Humidity, *see* Relative humidity

Illumination, *see* Daylighting; Electric lighting; Light
Infiltration:
    daily generic heating/cooling strategies, 57–58
    heat gain and loss estimation, 48
    solar heating and, 64
    window size and, 134
Inside temperature, 52–53. *See also* Cooling; Heating;
    Internal microclimate; Temperature
Insulation:
    bioclimatic design strategies, 50
    design strategies, 65
    earth sheltering, 87
    heat flow estimation, 44–45
    massive storage walls, 124

recommended levels, 44
roof ponds, 97
skin requirements for, 120
solar heat gain estimation, 46
solar heating by window size, 130–133
windows, 142–143
Interior reflectances, *see* Reflection
Internal heat gain, *see* Heat gain
Internal microclimate:
    bioclimatic chart approach, 34
    electric lighting heat gain, 40
    equipment heat gain, 41
    heat flow estimation, 44–45
    occupancy heat gain, 38–39
    solar heat gain, 46–47
    see also Microclimate phenomenon; Topographical
        microclimates

Landscaping, prevailing breeze room orientation, 90–91.
    See also Planting
Latent heat, 38
Light:
    daily heating cooling patterns, 57
    daylight availability curves, 32
    passive solar supplementation, 148–149
    plotting skycover approach, 30–31
    program and use, 37
    see also Daylighting; Electric lighting
Light shelves:
    thin building organization, 102
    windows, 140

Mashrabiyya (window screens), 72, 73
Masonry, 124
Materials:
    heat flow estimation, 44–45
    thermal mass, 51
Microclimate phenomenon:
    air movement principles, 26–27
    matrix of, 28
    topographical, 74
    see also Internal microclimate
Movable insulation, 142–143. *See also* Insulation

Natural ventilation, 51. *See also* Ventilation

Occupancy:
    daily generic heating/cooling strategies, 58
    internal heat gain estimation, 38–39
    program and use, 37

BUILDING INDEX

ARCHITECT INDEX

SELECTED TABLES, GRAPHS AND RULES OF THUMB INDEX

SELECTED TABLES, GRAPHS, AND RULES OF THUMB INDEX

175

SELECTED TABLES, GRAPHS, AND RULES OF THUMB INDEX